Learning Object-Oriented Programming, Design and TDD with Pharo

Stéphane Ducasse with Damien Pollet

April 1, 2018

master @ b7eb254

Layout and typography based on the sbabook LaTeX class by Damien Pollet.

Contents

Contents

Contents

Illustrations

CHAPTER 1

About this book

1.1 A word of presentation

I started to write this book back in 1998 when I wrote around 900 pages in preparation for *Learning Programming with Robots* (Apparently I needed to write to understand what I wanted to explain and how). From this I extracted *Learning Programming with Robots*, which was a book to teach simple concepts such as variables, loops, procedures and to help people teach kids how to program. My original objective was to write a second volum to teach object-oriented programming. But while this first volume was a success, I got really frustrated because to be understandable by everyone I had to remove what I like: object-oriented programming and good object-oriented design.

At that time, I met Harald Wertz, who gave me really nice ideas and pointers such as L-systems, then asked why I focused on procedural thinking and suggested that I should teach object-oriented programming instead. And he was right. This remark was like a bee in my bonnet for more than ten years. In fact, it was my original objective but I was exhausted after my first attempt and I had to focus on my academic life.

Now, nearly fifteen years later, I'm ready to write a book to start with object-oriented programming. In fact I rewrote everything I got from that time. I hope that you will enjoy it as much as I did — even if, for me, writing a book is a really long and daunting task because I want to make it great. I plan to write another volume on patterns of design that will extend this book.

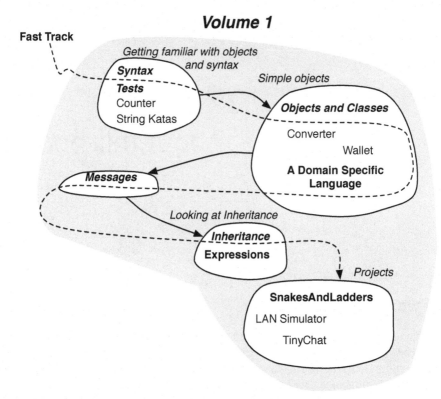

Figure 1-1   Reading maps.

1.2   Structure of the book

While writing this book, I faced a challenge to find the correct level of diffi-
culty. To solve this problem, I structured the book either into key chapters
on basic concepts, or into projects on more advanced topics. The projects
are little tutorials or more realistic examples, with step by step explana-
tions; you can skip over them and come back to read them whenever you feel
like it. I also propose various paths through the book with different levels of
reading; however, many of the *simpler* chapters also contain design remarks.

Fast track

The following chapters contain more conceptual information:

In the volume 1:

- Glimpse of the syntax

- Tests, tests and tests

- Objects and classes

- Revisiting objects and classes

- Domain specific language

- Inheritance and expressions

- Sending messages

- Snakes and ladders

The other chapters are more exercise and pratical. For example, with Tiny-Chat you will have fun with a web server written in the single page of code. You will find the solutions of the exercises in a separate pdf available on the book web site at http://books.pharo.org and the associated github repository https://github.com/SquareBracketAssociates/LearningOOPWithPharo.

1.3   What you will learn

I would like to present the concepts that I want to teach you and that hopefully you should acquire. What is key to understand is that I will focus on the *key* conceptual elements. It is easy for me because I will not explain OOP/D in general but within the context of Pharo and Pharo is the essence of Object-Oriented programming since its object model is minimal but it covers the key and essential aspect of OOP. For example we will not present method modifiers, types, overloading (which is a bad concept).

We will focus on object-oriented *programming* concepts:

- Objects / Classes

- Messages / Methods

- self and its semantics

- Inheritance

- super and its semantics

...and on object-oriented *design* concepts:

- Class responsibility collaboration

- Delegation

- Message sends are choice

- Message sends are plans for reuse

- The "Don't ask, tell" Principle

- Tests are your life ensurance

- Polymorphism

In addition we will also present

- Tests
- Software refactorings

Growing software

Often books present a problem and its solution. Now for non trivial problems, the solution does not fall from the sky or get developed in one stroke but it is the constant evolution of a first solution that evolves over time. Such an evolution is often difficult and tedious because the developer jumps from one stable state to a situation where his code may not work anymore. This is where Test Driven Design and refactorings really help. Test Driven Design helps focusing on new features and captures them as executable entities: tests. Refactorings helps by transforming code without breaking its invariants. Note that tests do not forbid to break code, they help identifying when previous invariants or constraints got violated. Sometimes violated tests identify a bug but they may be broken just because the requirements changed and that the tests should be updated. In this book, I wanted to see how software grows in little steps. This is what I do frequently during my coding sessions and I think that this is important to cover the hidden paths in software creation.

Syntax, blocks and iterators

Since we need a language to express our programs, we will teach you the syntax of Pharo. In particular we will use some simple chapters to get you started.

Now in a nutshell, you should know that the Pharo syntax

- fits in one postcard and
- is based on objects, messages and closures.

Note that closures are not a recent addition to the language but a central cornerstone. Closures are the foundation for conditional and loops. They enable this 'messages all over the place' syntax as well as really powerful iterators.

1.4 Typographic conventions

Pharo expressions or code snippets are represented either in the text as 'Hello' and 'Hello' reversed, or for more substantial snippets, as follows:

```
[ 'Hello'
```

When we want to show the result of evaluating an expression, we show the result after three chevrons >>> on the next line, like so:

```
'Hello' reversed
>>> 'olleH'
```

Whenever we feel the text makes a point that is important or technical enough to be highlighted, we will do so with a thick bar:

| Important   This is a point that is worth drawing some more attention.

Finally, the coffee cups highlight some points to take away and serve as a concise summary of the sections :

If you skim through a section, take a few seconds to check for coffee cups!

1.5   Videos

While reading this book you can also use some of the videos produced for the Pharo mooc. All the videos are available at http://mooc.pharo.org. I strongly suggest to watch the videos explaining how to use and interact with the environment.

1.6   Thanks

I would like to thanks Morgane Pigny, Anne Etien, Quentin Ducasse, Sven van Caekenberghe, Hayatou Oumarou, Kateryna Aloshkina, Ricardo Pacheco, Olivier Auverlot, Mariette Biernacki, Herby Vojcik, Denis Kudriashov, Holger Freyther, Dimitris Chloupis, Amal Noussi, René Paul Mages, Hannes Hirsel, Lorenzo Solano Martinez for their great feedback. Alexandre Bergel for his examples on messages. Olivier Auverlot for his constant enthousiam and for TinyChat. Guillermo Polito for the idea of file and directory example. Damien Pollet for this great template and the new LAN implementation and the numerous makefile implementation and Pillar help.

Part I

Getting in touch with Pharo

CHAPTER 2

Pharo syntax in a nutshell

In this chapter, we start on a simple path to get you to understand the most important parts of the Pharo syntax: *messages, blocks* and *methods.* This chapter is freely inspired from Sven van Caeckenberghe's gentle syntax introduction, and I thank him for giving me the permission to reuse his ideas.

In Pharo, everything is an *object* and computation happens by sending *messages* to objects. Objects are created by sending messages to particular objects named *classes,* which define the structure and behavior of the objects they create, also known as their instances.

2.1 Simplicity and elegance of messages

Messages are central to computation in Pharo. While their syntax is quite minimalist, it is very expressive and structures most of the language.

There are three kinds of messages: unary, binary, and keyword-based.

Sending a message & the receiver

Let's first look at an example of sending a message to an object:

```
'hello' reversed
```

What this means is that the message reversed is sent to the literal string 'hello'. In fact, the string 'hello' is called the *receiver* of the message; the receiver is always the leftmost part of a message.

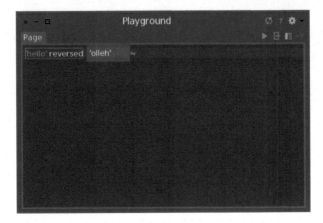

Figure 2-1 Executing an expression in Playground.

Evaluating code and convention for showing results

In Pharo, code can be evaluated from anywhere you can type and select text; the system provides various interactive ways to evaluate code and look at the result. In this book, we will show the result of an expression directly after it, using three chevrons >>>.

Evaluating the piece of code in the previous example yields a new string with the same characters in reverse order:

```
'hello' reversed
>>> 'olleh'
```

Figure 2-1 describes that we edited an expression and executed in with Playground.

Other messages & return values

Our 'hello' string understands many other messages than reversed:

```
'hello' asUppercase
>>> 'HELLO'
```

As the name implies, the asUppercase message returns yet another string 'HELLO', which has the same contents as the receiver with each character converted to upper case. However, messages sent to strings do not always return strings; other kinds of values are possible:

```
'hello' first
>>> $h

'hello' size
>>> 5
```

The message first returns the first element of the string: a character. Literal characters in Pharo syntax are expressed by the dollar sign $ immediately followed by the character itself. The message size returns the number of elements in the string, which is an integer.

Strings, characters, integers are objects, because in Pharo *everything* is an object. Also, messages *always* return something, even if the returned value is not used. One might say that a message can return any value, as long as it's an object.

The selector & unary messages

All messages we saw so far have the same receiver, the string 'hello'; however, the computations were different because the messages differ by their name, or to use the technical term, by their *selector*. In the syntax of a message, the selector always comes right after the receiver; the message-sending syntax is just the white space in between!

Those messages are called *unary* because they involve only one object: their receiver; they do not take any arguments. Syntactically, the selectors of unary messages must be alphabetic words; the convention to make up longer selectors is to use lower camel case, preferring asUppercase over as_uppercase or AsUPPERCASE.

A first keyword-based message

Messages often need to pass arguments to the receiver so that it can perform its task; this is what keyword-based messages are for.

As an example, instead of using first, we could use the message at:, with an explicit position as a parameter:

```
'hello' at: 1
>>>$h
```

The selector at: consists of a single keyword that ends with a colon, signifying that it should be followed by an argument; in this case, an integer indicating which element we want to access. Pharo counts indices starting from 1; therefore the message at: 2 will access the second element of the receiver.

```
'hello' at: 2
>>>$e
```

Keyword-based messages with multiple arguments

To pass more than one argument, a single message can have as many colon-terminated keywords as necessary, each followed by an argument, like this:

```
'hello' copyFrom: 1 to: 3
>>> 'hel'
```

This is one single message, whose selector is really copyFrom:to:. Note how naturally it reads and how, with well-chosen terms, each keyword of the selector documents the argument that follows it.

In the syntax, you are free to use as much white space as needed between the keywords and the arguments, and like unary messages, the convention is to name each keyword using lower camel case.

Binary messages

Binary messages visually differ from the other two kinds because their selectors can only be composed of symbols. They always expect a single argument, even though they do not end in a colon.

The main use of binary messages is as arithmetic operations, for instance sending the message + to the integer 1, with 2 as argument:

```
1 + 2
```

But there are some other widely-used binary messages outside of arithmetics; for example, the message (selector) for string concatenation is a single comma:

```
'Hello' , ' Pharoers'
>>> 'Hello Pharoers'
```

Here, the receiver is 'Hello' and ' Pharoers' is the argument.

☕ The *receiver* is the object to which a message is sent; it is always first in a message, followed by the *selector* and arguments.

☕ *Unary messages* look like words and have no parameters beside their receiver. *Binary messages* have selectors made of symbols and have one parameter. *Keyword messages* take a parameter after each colon in their selector.

☕ A message is composed of a receiver, a message name, called its selector and optional arguments. By language abuse, we sometimes use message when in fact we mean the selector of the message. , is a message selector and 'a' , 'b' is a message.

☕ The preferred naming convention for unary and keyword selectors is lower camel case, likeThis:orThat:.

2.2 Which message is executed first?

Simpler messages take precedence over the more complex ones. This very simple rule determines execution order when messages of different kinds appear in the same expression. This means that unary messages are evaluated first, then binary messages, and finally keyword-based messages.

Together, the message syntax and precedence rules keep complex expressions elegant and readable:

```
'string' asUppercase copyFrom: -1 + 2 to: 6 - 3
>>> STR
```

When message precedence does not match what you mean, you can force the execution order using parentheses. In the following example, the expression inside the parentheses is evaluated first; this yields a three-character string 'STR', which then receives the message reversed.

```
('string' asUppercase first: 9 / 3) reversed
>>> 'RTS'
```

Finally, note how copyFrom:to: and first: were sent to the result of asUppercase. All messages are expressions whose result can be the receiver of a subsequent message; this is called *message chaining*. Unless the precedence rule applies, chained messages execute in reading order, from left to right. This is quite natural for unary messages:

```
'abcd' allButFirst reversed
>>> 'dcb'

'abcd' reversed allButFirst
>>> 'cba'
```

Note however that the chaining rule applies without exception, even to binary messages that look like arithmetic operators:

```
1 + 2 * 10
>>> 30
```

Finally, keyword messages cannot be chained together without using parentheses, since the chain would look like a single big keyword message.

2.3   Sending messages to classes

Where do new objects come from? Well, in Pharo, object creation is just another form of computation, so it happens by sending a message to the class itself. For example, we can ask the class String to create an empty string by sending it the message new.

```
String new
>>> ''
```

Classes are really objects that are known by name, so they provide a useful entry point to the system; creating new objects is just a particular use-case. Some classes understand messages that return specific instances, like the class Float that understands the message pi.

```
Float pi
>>> 3.141592653589793
```

☕ The naming convention for class names is upper camel case, LikeThis; this is the convention for all non-local names, i.e. shared or global variables.

2.4 Local variables and statement sequences

Local variables are declared by writing their name between vertical bars; their value can be set using the assignment statement :=. Successive statements are *separated* using a period, which makes them look like sentences.

```
| anArray |
anArray := Array new: 3.
anArray at: 1 put: true.
anArray at: 2 put: false.
anArray
>>> #(true false nil)
```

In the code above, a new three-element array is created, and a reference to it is stored in anArray. Then, its first two elements are set using the at:put: message, leaving the last element uninitialized; indexing is one-based, like normal humans count.

The final statement determines the value of the whole sequence; it is shown using the syntax for literal arrays #(...). The first element is the boolean constant true, the second its counterpart false. Uninitialised elements remain nil, the undefined object constant.

☕ The first element of a collection is at index 1.

☕ The naming convention for local variables is lower camel case; variable names often start with an indefinite article, since they refer to otherwise anonymous objects.

☕ There are *only six reserved keywords*, and all are pseudo-variables: the true, false, and nil object constants, and self, super and thisContext, which we talk about later.

2.5 About literal objects

Most objects in Pharo are created programmatically, by sending a message like new to a class. In addition, the language syntax supports creating certain objects by directly expressing them in the code. For example the expression #(true false nil) is equivalent to the previous snippet using Array new.

In the same way, $A is equivalent to Character codePoint: 65:

```
Character codePoint: 65
>>> $A
```

2.6   Sending multiple messages to the same object

We often need to send multiple messages to the same receiver, in close succession. For instance, to build a long string without doing too many concatenations, we use a stream:

```
| aStream |
aStream := (String new: 100) writeStream.
aStream nextPutAll: 'Today, '.
aStream nextPutAll: Date today printString.
aStream contents
>>> 'Today, 28 January 2017'
```

Repeating aStream is tedious to read. To make this flow better, we group the three messages into a *message cascade*, separating them with semicolons, and stating the receiver only once at the beginning:

```
| aStream |
aStream := (String new: 100) writeStream.
aStream
  nextPutAll: 'Today, ';
  nextPutAll: Date today printString;
  contents
>>> 'Today, 28 January 2017'
```

Like with statement sequences, the cascade as a whole returns the value of its last message. Here is another example and its cascaded version:

```
| anArray |
anArray := Array new: 2.
anArray at: 1 put: true.
anArray at: 2 put: false.
anArray
>>> #(true false)
```

```
(Array new: 2)
  at: 1 put: true;
  at: 2 put: false;
  yourself
>>> #(true false)
```

The three indented messages form a cascade; they are all sent to the same object, the new array. The last message, yourself, is particularly useful to conclude cascades, because it returns the object it is sent to. This is necessary in this case because the at:put: message would return the assigned element, not the array.

2.7 Blocks

Square brackets [and] specify *blocks* (also known as lexical closures), pieces of code to be executed later on.

In the following example, the adder local variable is assigned a one argument block. The code inside the block describes the variables it accepts : x and the statements to be executed when it is evaluated x + 1. Evaluating a block is done by sending a message, value: with an actual object as argument. The argument gets bound to the variable and the block is executed, resulting in 101.

```
| adder |
adder := [ :x | x + 1 ].
adder value: 100
>>> 101
adder value: 200
>>> 201
```

> **Important** Blocks are technical lexical closures. Now in a first understanding, they represent kind of anonymous methods that can be sorted, passed as arguments and executed on demand using the messages value, value:...

2.8 Control structures

Blocks are used to express all control structures, from standard conditionals and loops to the exotic application specific ones, using the normal messaging syntax. For example loops and conditions are all expressed using the message presented previously. There are many loops and conditional in Pharo but they are all using the same principle: a block is passed as argument and the loop definition defines when the block should be executed.

The message timesRepeat: executes multiple time its argument (a block). Here we multiply by two a number 10 times.

```
n := 1.
10 timesRepeat: [ n := n * 2 ].
n
>>> 1024
```

Conditionals are expressed by sending one of the messages ifTrue:, ifFalse:, ifTrue:ifFalse:, or ifFalse:ifTrue: to the result of a boolean expression.

```
(17 * 13 > 220)
    ifTrue: [ 'bigger' ]
    ifFalse: [ 'smaller' ]
>>>'bigger'
```

16

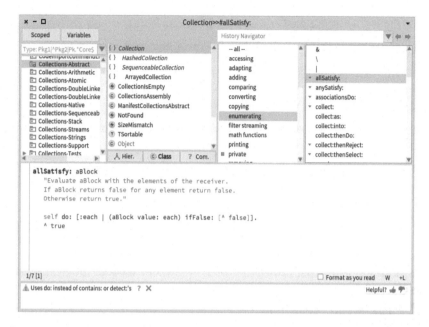

Figure 2-2 Reading or editing a method using a code browser. Topleft pane: list of packages then list of classes then protocols then method lists - middle pane: method definition. Last pane: Quality Assistant.

The message do: allows one to express a loop over a sequence of objects: a block is executed on each of the elements.

Let us see how we can count the number of character i in a given string. On each character we check if the character is an $i and increase the counter value if this is the case.

```
| count |
count := 0.
'Fear is the little-death that brings total obliteration'
    do: [:c | c == $i ifTrue: [count := count + 1]].
count
>>> 5
```

2.9 Methods

Imagine that we want the following behavior: checking that all the objects of a collection holds the given property.

Here we check that all the numbers in the array are even numbers.

```
#(2 4 8 16 32) allSatisfy: [ :each | each even ]
>>> true
```

But the following is false because not all the numbers are odd.

```
#(1 2 3 4 5 6) allSatisfy: [ :each | each odd ]
>>> false
```

The message allSatisfy: is one of the many super powerful behavior implemented in Collection. It is called an iterator.

Methods are edited one by one in a code browser, like the one shown in Figure 2-2.

The following code is the definition of the method allSatisfy:. The first line specifies the method name, the selector, with names for all arguments. Comments are surrounded by double quotes. Inside a method, self refers to the object itself, the receiver.

Let us explain the implementation of such method. Using the message do: we iterate over all elements of the collection. For each element we execute block (a predicate) that returns a boolean value and act accordingly. As soon as we get a false value, we stop and return an overall false value. If every evaluation gave us true, we passed the whole test and can return true as overall result.

```
allSatisfy: aBlock
  "Evaluate aBlock with the elements of the receiver.
  If aBlock returns false for any element return false.
  Otherwise return true."
  self do: [:each | (aBlock value: each) ifFalse: [^ false]].
  ^ true
```

In a method, the receiver (self) is the default return value of the whole method. Using a caret (^) a method returns something else or even return earlier. Here is the code of the method allSatify: on the class Collection.

2.10 Resources

This chapter showed you the key syntatic elements. If you want to get a deeper understanding about the syntax please refer to the following mooc videos. The Mooc on Pharo is available at http://mooc.pharo.org

Here are direct pointers to the videos we believe will help you to understand the Pharo syntax and key messages:

- Syntax in a nutshell http://rmod-pharo-mooc.lille.inria.fr/MOOC/Videos/ W1/C019SD-W1-S5-v2.mp4

- Understanding messages http://rmod-pharo-mooc.lille.inria.fr/MOOC/ Videos/W2/C019SD-W2-S1-v3.mp4

- Pharo for the Java Programmer http://rmod-pharo-mooc.lille.inria.fr/ MOOC/Videos/W2/C019SD-W2-S2-v3.mp4

- Message precedence http://rmod-pharo-mooc.lille.inria.fr/MOOC/Videos/W2/C019SD-W2-S3-v3.mp4

- Sequence and cascade http://rmod-pharo-mooc.lille.inria.fr/MOOC/Videos/W2/C019SD-W2-S3-v3.mp4

- Blocks http://rmod-pharo-mooc.lille.inria.fr/MOOC/Videos/W2/C019SD-W2-S6-v2.mp4

- Loops http://rmod-pharo-mooc.lille.inria.fr/MOOC/Videos/W2/C019SD-W2-S7-v2.mp4

- Booleans and collections http://rmod-pharo-mooc.lille.inria.fr/MOOC/Videos/W2/C019SD-W2-S8-v2.mp4

- Class and Method Definition http://rmod-pharo-mooc.lille.inria.fr/MOOC/Videos/W1/C019SD-W1-S6-v3.mp4

- Understanding return http://rmod-pharo-mooc.lille.inria.fr/MOOC/Videos/W3/C019SD-W3-S11-v1.mp4

- Parentheses http://rmod-pharo-mooc.lille.inria.fr/MOOC/Videos/W2/C019SD-W2-S9-v3.mp4

- Yourself http://rmod-pharo-mooc.lille.inria.fr/MOOC/Videos/W2/C019SD-W2-S10-v3.mp4

- Variables http://rmod-pharo-mooc.lille.inria.fr/MOOC/Videos/W3/C019SD-W3-S3-v3.mp4

- Essential collections http://rmod-pharo-mooc.lille.inria.fr/MOOC/Videos/W3/C019SD-W3-S7-v3.mp4

- Iterators http://rmod-pharo-mooc.lille.inria.fr/MOOC/Videos/W3/C019SD-W3-S9-v3.mp4

2.11   Conclusion

You have three kinds of messages and the simpler are executed prior to more complex one. Hence unary messages are executed before binary and binary before keyword-based messages. Blocks are anonymous methods that can be pass around and used to define control structures and loops.

You now know enough to read 95% of Pharo code. Remember, it is all just messages being sent to objects.

CHAPTER 3

Syntax summary

Six reserved words only

`nil`	the undefined object
`true, false`	boolean objects
`self`	the receiver of the current message
`super`	the receiver, in the superclass context
`thisContext`	the current invocation on the call stack

Reserved syntactic constructs

`"comment"`	comment
`'string'`	string
`#symbol`	unique string
`$a`, Character space	the character a and a space
`12 2r1100 16rC`	twelve (decimal, binary, hexadecimal)
`3.14 1.2e3`	floating-point numbers
`#( abc 123 )`	literal array with the symbol #abc and the number 123
`{foo . 3 + 2}`	dynamic array built from 2 expressions
`#[123 21 255]`	byte array
exp1. exp2	expression separator (period)
`;`	message cascade (semicolon)
var := *expr*	assignment
^ *expr*	return a result from a method (caret)
`[:e	expr]`	code block with a parameter
`| var1 var2 |`	declaration of two temporary variables

Message Sending

When we send a message to an object, the message *receiver*, the method is selected and executed; the message returns an object. Messages syntax mimics natural languages, with a subject, a verb, and complements.

Java	Pharo
`aColor.setRGB(0.2,0.3,0)`	`aColor r: 0.2 g: 0.3 b: 0`
`d.put("1", "Chocolate");`	`d at: '1' put: 'Chocolate'`

Three Types of Messages: Unary, Binary, and Keyword

A **unary** message is one with no arguments.

```
Array new
>>> anArray
```

```
#(4 2 1) size
>>> 3
```

new is an unary message sent to classes (classes are objects).

A **binary** message takes only one argument and is named by one or more symbol characters from +, -, *, = , <, >, ...

```
3 + 4
>>> 7
```

```
'Hello' , ' World'
>>>'Hello World'
```

The + message is sent to the object 3 with 4 as argument. The string 'Hello' receives the message , (comma) with ' World' as the argument.

A **keyword** message can take one or more arguments that are inserted in the message name.

```
'Pharo' allButFirst: 2==
>>> 'aro'
```

```
3 to: 10 by: 2
>>> (3 to: 10 by: 2)
```

The second example sends to:by: to 3, with arguments 10 and 2; this returns an interval containing 3, 5, 7, and 9.

Message Precedence

Parentheses > unary > binary > keyword, and finally from left to right.

```
(15 between: 1 and: 2 + 4 * 3) not
>>> false
```

Messages + and * are sent first, then between:and: is sent, and not. The rule suffers no exception: operators are just binary messages with *no notion of mathematical precedence.* 2 + 4 * 3 reads left-to-right and gives 18, not 14!

Cascade: Sending Muliple Messages to the Same Object

Multiple messages can be sent to the same receiver with ;.

```
OrderedCollection new
   add: #abc;
   add: #def;
   add: #ghi.
```

The message new is sent to OrderedCollection which returns a new collection to which three add: messages are sent. The value of the whole message cascade is the value of the last message sent (here, the symbol #ghi). To return the receiver of the message cascade instead (i.e. the collection), make sure to send yourself as the last message of the cascade.

Blocks

Blocks are objects containing code that is executed on demand. They are the basis for control structures like conditionals and loops.

```
2 = 2
   ifTrue: [ Error signal: 'Help' ]
```

```
#('Hello World')
   do: [ :e | Transcript show: e ]
```

The first example sends the message ifTrue: to the boolean true (computed from 2 = 2) with a block as argument. Because the boolean is true, the block is executed and an exception is signaled. The next example sends the message do: to an array. This evaluates the block once for each element, passing it via the e parameter. As a result, Hello World is printed.

Common Constructs: Conditionals

In Java

```
if (condition)
   { action(); }
   else { anotherAction();}
```

In Pharo

```
condition
   ifTrue: [ action ]
   ifFalse: [ anotherAction ]
```

In Java

```
while (condition) { action();
    anotherAction(); }
```

In Pharo

```
[ condition ] whileTrue: [ action. anotherAction ]
```

Common Constructs: Loops/Iterators

In Java

```
for(int i=1; i<11; i++){
    System.out.println(i); }
```

In Pharo

```
1 to: 11 do: [ :i | Transcript show: i ; cr ]
```

In Java

```
String [] names ={"A", "B", "C"};
for( String name : names ) {
    System.out.print( name );
    System.out.print(","); }
```

In Pharo

```
| names |
names := #('A' 'B' 'C').
names do: [ :each | Transcript show: each, ' , ' ]
```

Collections start at 1. Messages at: index gives element at index and at: index put: value sets element at index to value.

```
#(4 2 1) at: 3
>>> 1
```

```
#(4 2 1) at: 3 put: 6
>>>#(4 2 6)
```

```
Set new add: 4; add: 4; yourself
>>> aSet
```

Files and Streams

```
work := FileSystem disk workingDirectory.
stream := (work / 'foo.txt') writeStream.
stream nextPutAll: 'Hello World'.
stream close.
stream := (work / 'foo.txt') readStream.
stream contents.
>>> 'Hello World'
stream close.
```

CHAPTER 4

Challenge yourself

In Pharo everything is an object and most computation happens by sending *messages* to objects. In this chapter we propose a list of exercises to challenge you with the syntax.

4.1 Challenge: Message identification

For each of the expressions below, fill in the answers:

- What is the receiver object?
- What is the message selector?
- What is/are the argument (s)?
- What is the result returned by this expression execution?

```
3 + 4

receiver:
selector:
arguments:
result:
```

```
Date today

receiver:
selector:
arguments:
result:
```

```
#('' 'World') at: 1 put: 'Hello'

  receiver:
  selector:
  arguments:
  result:
```

```
#(1 22 333) at: 2

  receiver:
  selector:
  arguments:
  result:
```

```
#(2 33 -4 67) collect: [ :each | each abs ]

  receiver:
  selector:
  arguments:
  result:
```

```
25 @ 50

  receiver:
  selector:
  arguments:
  result:
```

```
SmallInteger maxVal


  receiver:
  selector:
  arguments:
  result:
```

```
#(a b c d e f) includesAll: #(f d b)

  receiver:
  selector:
  arguments:
  result:
```

```
true | false

  receiver:
  selector:
  arguments:
  result:
```

```
Point selectors

    receiver:
    selector:
    arguments:
    result:
```

4.2 Challenge: Literal objects

What kind of object does the following literal expressions refer to? It is the same as asking what is the result of sending the class message to such expressions.

```
1.3

>
```

```
#node1

>
```

```
#(2 33 4)

>
```

```
'Hello, Dave'

>
```

```
[ :each | each scale: 1.5 ]

>
```

```
$A

>
```

```
true

>
```

```
1

>
```

4.3 Challenge: Kind of messages

Examine the following messages and report if the message is unary, binary or keyword-based.

```
┌ 1 log
│
└ >

┌ Browser open
│
└ >

┌ 2 raisedTo: 5
│
└ >

┌ 'hello', 'world'
│
└ >

┌ 10@20
│
└ >

┌ point1 x
│
└ >

┌ point1 distanceFrom: point2
│
└ >
```

4.4 Challenge: Results

Examine the following expressions. What is the value returned by the execution of the following expressions?

```
┌ 1 + 3 negated
│
└ >

┌ 1 + (3 negated)
│
└ >

┌ 2 raisedTo: 3 + 2
│
└ >

┌ | anArray |
│ anArray := #('first' 'second' 'third' 'fourth').
│ anArray at: 2
│
│
└ >
```

```
#(2 3 -10 3) collect: [ :each | each * each]
>
```

```
6 + 4 / 2
>
```

```
2 negated raisedTo: 3 + 2
>
```

```
#(a b c d e f) includesAll: #(f d b)
>
```

4.5 Challenge: unneeded parentheses

Putting more parentheses than necessary is a good way to get started. Such practice however leads to less readable expressions. Rewrite the following expressions using the least number of parentheses.

```
x between: (pt1 x) and: (pt2 y)


    ...
```

```
((#(a b c d e f) asSet) intersection: (#(f d b) asSet))


    ...
```

```
(x isZero)
    ifTrue: [....]
(x includes: y)
    ifTrue: [....]




    ...
```

```
(OrderedCollection new)
    add: 56;
    add: 33;
    yourself
```

```
 ...

((3 + 4) + (2 * 2) + (2 * 3))


 ...

(Integer primesUpTo: 64) sum


 ...

('http://www.pharo.org' asUrl) retrieveContents


 ...
```

CHAPTER 5

Developing a simple counter

To get started in Pharo, we invite you to implement a simple counter by following the steps given below. In this exercise you will learn how to create packages classes, methods, instances. You will learn how to define tests and more. This simple tutorial covers most of the important actions that we do when developing in Pharo.

Note that the development flow promoted by this little tutorial is *traditional* in the sense that you will define a package, a class, *then* define its instance variable *then* define its methods *and* finally execute it. The companion video follows also such programming development flow. Now in Pharo, developers often follow a *totally* different style (that we call live coding) where they execute an expression that raises errors and they code in the debugger and let the system define some instance variables and methods on the fly for them. Once you will have finished this tutorial, you will feel more confident with Pharo and we strongly suggest you to try the other style by following the second video showing such different development practices.

5.1 Our use case

Here is our use case: we want to be able to create a counter, increment it twice, decrement it and check that its value is correct. It looks like this little use case will fit perfectly a unit test - you will define one later.

```
| counter |
counter := Counter new.
counter increment; increment.
counter decrement.
counter count = 1
```

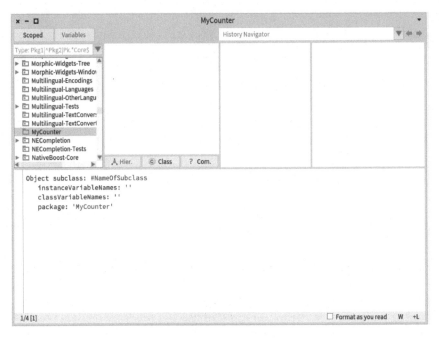

Figure 5-1 Package created and class creation template.

Now we will develop all the mandatory class and methods to support this scenario.

5.2 Create your own class

In this part, you will create your first class. In Pharo, a class is defined in a package. You will create a package then a class. The steps we will do are the same ones every time you create a class, so memorize them well.

Create a package

Using the Browser create a package. The system will ask you a name, write MyCounter. This new package is then created and added to the list. Figure 5-1 shows the result of creating such a package.

Create a class

Creating a class requires four steps. They consist basically in editing the class definition template to specify the class you want to create.

- By default, the system helps you to define a subclass of the class Object. This is why it is written Object subclass: #NameOfSubclass.

- **Class Name.** You should fill in the name of your class by replacing the word NameOfSubclass with the word Counter. Take care that the name of the class starts with a capital letter and that you do not remove the #sign in front of NameOfClass. This is because the class we want to create does not exist yet, so we have to give its name, and we use a Symbol (a unique string in Pharo) to do so.

- **Instance variable definition.** Then, you should fill in the names of the instance variables of this class. We need one instance variable called count. Take care that you leave the string quotes!

- **Class variable definition.** As we do not need any class variable make sure that the argument for the class instance variables is an empty string classInstanceVariableNames: ''.

You should get the following class definition.

```
Object subclass: #Counter
    instanceVariableNames: 'count'
    classVariableNames: ''
    package: 'MyCounter'
```

Now we should compile it. We now have a filled-in class definition for the class Counter. To define it, we still have to *compile* it. Therefore, select the accept menu item. The class Counter is now compiled and immediately added to the system.

Figure 5-2 illustrates the resulting situation that the browser should show.

The tool runs automatically some code critic and some of them are just inaccurate, so do not care for now.

As we are disciplined developers, we add a comment to Counter class by clicking Comment button. You can write the following comment:

```
Counter is a simple concrete class which supports incrementing and
    decrementing a counter.
Its API is
- decrement, increment
- count
Its creation API is message withValue:
```

Select menu item 'accept' to store this class comment in the class.

5.3 Define protocols and methods

In this part you will use the browser to learn how to add protocols and methods.

The class we have defined has one instance variable named count. You should remember that in Pharo, (1) everything is an object, (2) instance variables

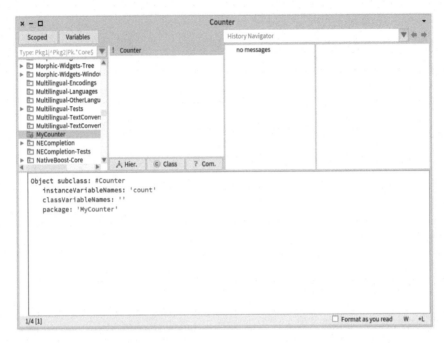

Figure 5-2 Class created.

are private to the object, and (3) the only way to interact with an object is by sending messages to it.

Therefore, there is no other mechanism to access the instance variable values from outside an object than sending a message to the object. What you can do is to define messages that return the value of the instance variable. Such methods are called *accessors*, and it is a common practice to always define and use them. We start to create an accessor method for our instance variable count.

A method is usually sorted into a protocol. These protocols are just a group of methods without any language semantics, but convey important navigation information for the reader of your class. You get protocol named: 'testing' for method performing tests, 'printing' for methods displaying the object, 'accessing' for simple accessor methods and so on.

Although protocols can have any name, Pharo programmers follow certain conventions for naming these protocols. But don't be stressed if you do not name well your protocols.

Create a method

Now let us create the accessor methods for the instance variable count. Start by selecting the class Counter in a browser, and make sure that you are editing the instance side of the class (i.e., we define methods that will be sent to instances) by deselecting the Class side radio button.

Create a new protocol by bringing the menu of methods protocol list: click on the third list from the left. Select the newly created protocol. Then in the bottom pane, the edit field displays a method template laying out the default structure of a method. As a general hint, double click at the end of or beginning of the text and start typing your method. Replace the template with the following method definition:

```
count
    "return the current value of the value instance variable"
    ^ count
```

This defines a method called count, taking no arguments, having a method comment and returning the instance variable count. Then choose *accept* in the menu to compile the method. You can now test your new method by typing and evaluating the next expression in a Playground, or any text editor.

```
Counter new count
>>> nil
```

This expression first creates a new instance of Counter, and then sends the message count to it. It retrieves the current value of the counter. This should return nil (the default value for non-initialised instance variables). Afterwards we will create instances with a reasonable default initialisation value.

Adding a setter method

Another method that is normally used besides the accessor method is a so-called setter method. Such a method is used to change the value of an instance variable from a client. For example, the expression Counter new count: 7 first creates a new Counter instance and then sets its value to 7:

The snippets shows that the counter effectively contains its value.

```
| c |
c := Counter new count: 7.
c count
>>> 7
```

This setter method does not currently exist, so as an exercise write the method count: such that, when invoked on an instance of Counter, instance variable is set to the argument given to the message. Test your method by typing and evaluating the expression above.

5.4 Define a Test Class

Writing tests is an important activity that will support the evolution of your application. Remember that a test is written *once and executed million* times. For example if we have turned the expression above into a test we could have checked automatically that our new method is correctly working.

To define a test case we will define a class that inherits from TestCase. Therefore define a class named CounterTest as follows:

```
TestCase subclass: #CounterTest
    instanceVariableNames: ''
    classVariableNames: ''
    package: 'MyCounter'
```

Now we can write a first test by defining one method. Test methods should start with *test* to be automatically executed by the TestRunner or when you press on the icon of the method. Now to make sure that you understand in which class we define the method we prefix the method body with the class name and >>. CounterTest>> means that the method is defined in the class CounterTest.

Define the following method. It first creates an instance, sets its value and verifies that the value is correct. The message assert: is a special message verifying if the test passed or not.

```
CounterTest >> testCountIsSetAndRead
    | c |
    c := Counter new.
    c count: 7.
    self assert: c count = 7
```

Verify that the test passes by executing either pressing the icon in front of the method or using the TestRunner available in the Tools menu (selecting your package). Since you have a first green test. This is a good moment to save your work.

5.5 Saving your work

Several ways to save your work exist.

- *Using plain files.* You can save the class or a method by clicking on it and selecting the fileout menu item. You will get a file containing the source code on your hard-disk - This is not the favorite way to save your code.

- *Using a version control system.* It is better to use a version control system. In Pharo you can use Monticello and Git (even if it is more for advanced users).

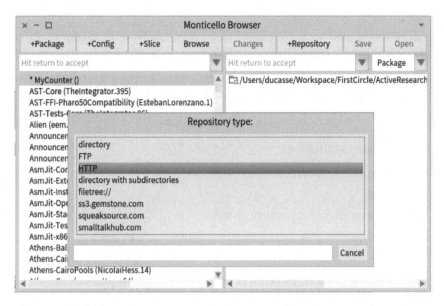

Figure 5-3 Selecting a new kind of repository to the list of possible places to commit the package.

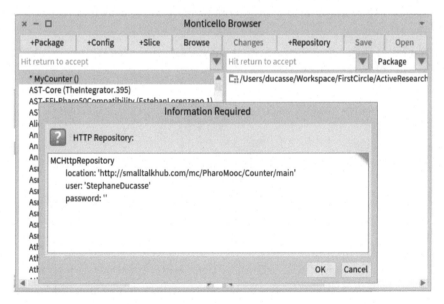

Figure 5-4 Editing the repository information.

In this chapter, we explain the simplest way to get you done. Note that the complete set of Pharo packages is managed via Monticello (which is a distributed versioning control system - there are chapters in **Pharo by Example** and **Deep into Pharo** books http://books.pharo.org).

Use the **Monticello Browser** (available in Tools) to save your work. You can save a package locally on your hard-disk or on a remote server on the web such as http://www.smalltalkhub.com

Saving using Monticello

Using Monticello you can save your work:

- *Locally*. You can store your packages in a folder on your disc (use directory as a kind of repository below).

- *Remotely*. Using an account on a free server such http://www.smalltalkhub.com/. You can save your work and share it with others.

Note each time you load or save a package, this package is also be stored in the folder named 'package-cache' on your hard-disk.

Add a repository

Go to http://www.smalltalkhub.com/ and create a member account then register a new project. You get an HTTP entry that refers to your project. Define a new HTTP repository using the Monticello Browser as shown by Figures 5-3 and 5-4.

Figure 5-3 shows that you package is dirty: this is indicated with the little '*' in front of the packages.

Example. As authors we are saving the examples for this chapter as a special team named PharoMooc in the Counter project so our information is the following:

```
MCHttpRepository
  location: 'http://smalltalkhub.com/mc/PharoMooc/Counter/main'
  user: ''
  password: ''
```

Now for you, you should adapt the following template to use your own information:

```
MCHttpRepository
  location: 'http://smalltalkhub.com/mc/YourAccount/YourProject/main'
  user: 'YourAccountID'
  password: 'YourAccountPassword'
```

Saving your package

To save your work, simply select your package and the repository you want to save it to and save it using the Save button. This will open a dialog where you can give a comment, version numbers and blessing. From then on, other people can load it from there, in the same way that you would use cvs or other multi-user versioning systems. Saving the image is also a way to save your working environment, but not a way to version and publish it in a way that can be easily shared.

You can of course both publish your package (so that other people can load it, and that you can compare it with other versions, etc.) and save your image (so that next time that you start your image you are in the same working environment).

5.6 **Adding more messages**

Before implementing the following messages we define first a test. We define one test for the method increment as follows:

```
CounterTest >> testIncrement
    | c |
    c := Counter new.
    c count: 0 ; increment; increment.
    self assert: c count = 2
```

Here we create a counter, set its value to 0, send it the message increment two times and verify that we get a counter of value 2.

Now you should implement some more methods.

- Propose a definition for the method increment and implement it.

- Implement also a new test method for the method decrement.

- Define the method decrement place it together with increment in the protocol 'operation'.

Here are the possible definitions for such methods.

```
Counter >> increment
    count := count + 1
```

```
Counter >> decrement
    count := count - 1
```

Run your tests they should pass (as shown in Figure 5-5). Again this is a good moment to save your work. Saving at point where tests are green is always a good process.

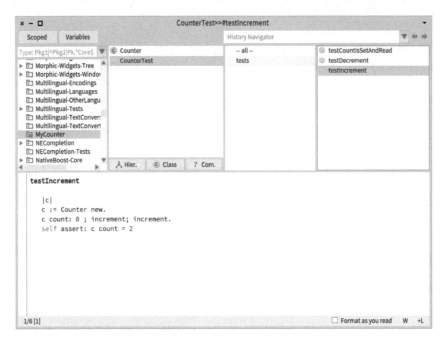

Figure 5-5 Class with green tests.

5.7 Better object description

When you select the expression `Counter new` and print its result (using the Print it menu of the editor) you obtain a simple string `'a Counter'`.

```
Counter new
>>> a Counter
```

We would like to get a much richer information for example knowing the counter value. Implement the following methods in the protocol `printing`

```
Counter >> printOn: aStream
    super printOn: aStream.
    aStream nextPutAll: ' with value: ', self count printString.
```

Note that the method `printOn:` is used when you print an object using print it (See Figure 5-6). In addition this method is invoked when you click on `self` in an inspector. An inspector is an object to interact and modify objects. It is really powerful during development.

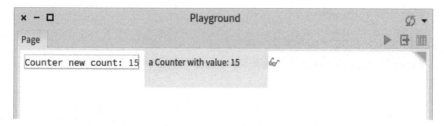

Figure 5-6   Better description doing a Print It (cmd + P).

5.8   Instance initialization method

Right now the initial value of our counter is not set as the following expression shows it.

```
Counter new count
>>> nil
```

Let us write a test checking that a newly created instance has 0 as a default value.

```
CounterTest >> testValueAtCreationTimeIsZero
    self assert: Counter new count = 0
```

If you run it, it will turn yellow indicating a failure (a situation that you anticipated but that is not correct) - by opposition to an error which is an anticipated situation leading to failed assertion.

Define an initialize method

Now we have to write an initialization method that sets a default value of the count instance variable. However, as we mentioned the initialize message is sent to the newly created instance. This means that the initialize method should be defined at the instance side as any method that is sent to an instance of Counter (like increment) and decrement. The initialize method is responsible to set up the default value of instance variables.

Therefore at the instance side, you should create a protocol initialization, and create the following method (the body of this method is left blank. Fill it in!).

```
Counter >> initialize
    "set the initial value of the value to 0"

    count := 0
```

Now create a new instance of class Counter. Is it initialized by default? The following code should now work without problem:

```
Counter new increment
```

and the following one should return 2

```
Counter new increment; increment; count
>>> 2
```

Again save your work

5.9 Conclusion

In this chapter you learned how to define packages, classes, methods, and define tests. The flow of programming that we chose for this first tutorial is similar to most of programming languages. In Pharo you can use a different flow that is based on defining a test first, executing it and when the execution raises error to define the corresponding classes, methods, and instance variables often from inside the debugger. We suggest you now to redo the exercise following the second companion video.

CHAPTER 6

Tests, tests and tests

In this chapter we start by showing that tests are simple. Second we present test driven design - basically what we will try to do systematically in this book. Then we discuss why we test, and what makes a good test. We then present a series of small examples showing how to use SUnit.

6.1 Writing a test in 2 minutes

A test is a context, a stimulus and an assertion (verification that we get the correct state). Here is an example on sets. Remember that sets are mathematical entities having only one occurrence of their elements.

First we test that adding an element changes the size of the set.

- **Context:** we take an empty set.
- **Stimulus:** we add $A into the empty set.
- **Assertion:** the set has one element.

Another test is that a set only contains only one occurence of one element.

- **Context:** we take an empty set.
- **Stimulus:** we add $A into the empty set.
- **Assertion:** the set has one element.
- **Stimulus:** we add $A into the empty set.
- **Assertion:** the set has still one element.

How do we declare a test in Pharo?

This is really easy to declare one test: we define one class (that will host multiple test definitions) and one method per test.

Here the class `MyExampleSetTest` should inherit from `TestCase`. It is the place to define the tests related to the class `Set`.

```
TestCase subclass: #MyExampleSetTest
    instanceVariableNames: ''
    classVariableNames: ''
    package: 'MySetTest'
```

Now we can define one test expression as a method. There is one constraint: the method selector should start with `test`.

```
MyExampleSetTest >> testAddTwice
    | s |
    s := Set new.
    self assert: s isEmpty.
    s add: $A.
    self assert: s size equals: 1.
    s add: $A.
    self assert: s size equals: 1.
```

Then using the Test runner or pressing on icons of the Pharo browser (as shown in Figure 6-1), you will be able to execute the method `testAddTwice` and it will tell you if it passes or fails (i.e., if its assertions are true). Now that you know that writing a test is not complex. Let us look a bit at the theory before going into more details.

☕ A test is a context, a stimulus and an *assertion* (verification that we get the correct state).

6.2 Test Driven Design

The interest in testing and Test Driven Development is not limited to Pharo. Automated testing has become a hallmark of the *Agile software development* movement, and any software developer concerned with improving software quality would do well to adopt it. Indeed, developers in many languages have come to appreciate the power of unit testing.

Neither testing, nor the building of test suites, is new. By now, everybody knows that tests are a good way to catch errors. By making testing a core practice and by emphasizing *automated* tests, Extreme Programming has helped to make testing productive and fun, rather than a chore that programmers dislike.

The Pharo community has a long tradition of testing because of the incremental style of development supported by its programming environment. In traditional Pharo development, a programmer writes tests in a playground as soon as a method was finished. Sometimes a test would be incorporated as a comment at the head of the method that it exercised, or tests that needed some set up would be included as example methods in the class. The problem with these practices is that tests in a playground are not available to other programmers who modify the code. Comments and example methods are better in this respect, but there is still no easy way to keep track of them and to run them automatically. Tests that are not run do not help you to find bugs! Moreover, an example method does not inform the reader of the expected result: you can run the example and see the (perhaps surprising) result, but you will not know if the observed behaviour is correct.

Using a testing framework such as SUnit is valuable because it allows us to write tests that are self-checking: the test itself defines what the correct result should be. It also helps us (1) to organize tests into groups, (2) to describe the context in which the tests must run, and (3) to run a group of tests automatically. As you saw, in less than two minutes you can write tests using SUnit, so instead of writing small code snippets in a playground, we encourage you to use SUnit and get all the advantages of stored and automatically executable tests.

6.3 Why testing is important

Now that you see that writing tests is simple. Let's step back and analyze the situation. Unfortunately, many developers believe that tests are a waste of their time. After all, *they* do not write bugs, only *other* programmers do that. Most of us have said, at some time or other: *I would write tests if I had more time.* If you never write a bug, and if your code will never be changed in the future, then indeed tests are a waste of your time. However, this most likely also means that your application is trivial, or that it is not used by you or anyone else. Think of tests as an investment for the future: having a test suite is quite useful now, but it will be *extremely* useful when your application, or the environment in which it runs, changes in the future.

Tests play several roles:

- First, they provide documentation of the functionality that they cover. This documentation is active: watching the tests pass tells you that the documentation is up to date.

- Second, tests help developers to confirm that some changes that they have just made to a package have not broken anything else in the system, and to find the parts that break when that confidence turns out to be misplaced.

- Finally, writing tests during, or even before, programming forces you to think about the functionality that you want to design, *and how it should appear to the client code*, rather than about how to implement it.

By writing the tests first, i.e., before the code, you are compelled to state the context in which your functionality will run, the way it will interact with the client code, and the expected results. Your code style will definitively improve.

Several software development methodologies such as *eXtreme Programming* and Test-Driven Development (TDD) advocate writing tests before writing code. This may seem to go against your deep instincts as software developers. All we can say is: go ahead and try it. Writing the tests before the code helps you know what we want to code, helps you know when you are done, and helps us conceptualize the functionality of a class and to design its interface. Moreover, test-first development gives you the courage to change our application, because you will know when you break something.

We cannot test all aspects of any realistic application. Covering a complete application is simply impossible and is the goal of testing. Even with a good test suite some bugs will still creep into the application, where they can lay dormant waiting for an opportunity to damage your system. If you find that this has happened, take advantage of it! As soon as you uncover the bug, write a test that exposes it, run the test, and watch it fail. Now you can start to fix the bug: the test will tell you when you are done.

6.4   What makes a good test?

Writing good tests is a skill that you can learn by practicing. Let us look at the properties that tests should have to get the maximum benefit.

- *Tests should be repeatable.* You should be able to run a test as often as you want, and always get the same answer.

- *Tests should run without human intervention.* You should be able to run them unattended.

- *Tests should tell a story.* Each test should cover one aspect of a piece of code. A test should act as a scenario that you or someone else can read to understand a piece of functionality.

- *Tests should have a change frequency lower than that of the functionality they cover.* You do not want to have to change all your tests every time you modify your application. One way to achieve this is to write tests based on the public interfaces of the class that you are testing. It is OK to write a test for a private *helper* method if you feel that the method is complicated enough to need the test, but you should be aware that such a test may have to be changed, or thrown away entirely, when you think of a better implementation.

One consequence of such properties is that the number of tests should be somewhat proportional to the number of functions to be tested: changing one aspect of the system should not break all the tests but only a limited number. This is important because having 100 tests fail should send a much stronger message than having 10 tests fail. However, it is not always possible to achieve this ideal: in particular, if a change breaks the initialization of an object, or the set-up of a test, it is likely to cause all of the tests to fail.

Now let's go back and write a couple of tests using SUnit.

6.5 SUnit by example

We show a step by step example. We continue with the example that tests the class Set. Try editing and compiling the code as we go along.

Pay attention: test classes are special classes. As subclasses of TestCase they have a different behavior that normal classes: their methods which start with test are automatically executed on newly created instances of the class. This is what happens when you press the icon close to the method in a class browser (as shown in Figure 6-1).

Step 1: Create the test class

We use the class MyExampleSetTest to group all the tests related to the class Set. First you should create a new subclass of TestCase called MyExample-SetTest.

```
TestCase subclass: #MyExampleSetTest
    instanceVariableNames: ''
    classVariableNames: ''
    package: 'MySetTest'
```

Step 2: Write a test method

Let's create some tests by defining some methods in the class MyExample-SetTest. Each method represents one test. The names of the methods should start with the string 'test' so that SUnit collects them into test suites. Test methods take no arguments.

Define the following test method named testIncludes. It tests the in-cludes: method of class Set. The test says that sending the message in-cludes: 5 to a set containing 5 should return true.

```
MyExampleSetTest >> testIncludes
    | full |
    full := Set with: 5 with: 6.
    self assert: (full includes: 5).
    self assert: (full includes: 6)
```

As you see this is quite simple. Let's continue.

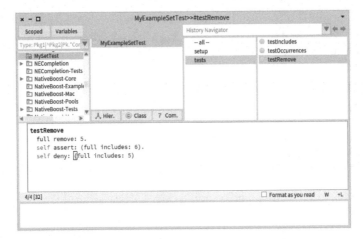

Figure 6-1 Running SUnit tests from the System Browser: Just click on the round little button close to the class or method.

Step 3: Run the test

The easiest way to run the tests is directly from the browser. Simply click on the icon of the class name, or on an individual test method, or use the *Run tests (t)* . The test methods will be flagged green or red, depending on whether they pass or not (as shown in Figure 6-1).

Step 4: Write more tests

Let's create more tests by defining some methods in the class MyExample-SetTest.

The second test, named testOccurrences, verifies that the number of occurrences of 5 in full set is equal to one, even if we add another element 5 to the set.

```
MyExampleSetTest >> testOccurrences
  | empty full |
  empty := Set new.
  full := Set with: 5 with: 6.
  self assert: (empty occurrencesOf: 0) equals: 0.
  self assert: (full occurrencesOf: 5) equals: 1.
  full add: 5.
  self assert: (full occurrencesOf: 5) equals: 1
```

Finally, we test that the set no longer contains the element 5 after we have removed it.

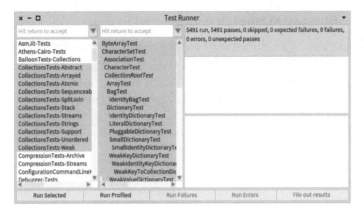

Figure 6-2   Running SUnit tests using the *TestRunner*.

```
MyExampleSetTest >> testRemove
  | full |
  full := Set with: 5 with: 6.
  full remove: 5.
  self assert: (full includes: 6).
  self deny: (full includes: 5)
```

Note the use of the method TestCase >> deny: to assert something that should not be true. aTest deny: anExpression is equivalent to aTest assert: anExpression not, but is much more readable.

Step 5: Run all the tests

You can also select sets of test suites to run, and obtain a more detailed log of the results using the SUnit Test Runner, which you can open by selecting the menu World > Test Runner.

The *Test Runner*, shown in Figure 6-2, is designed to make it easy to execute groups of tests.

The left-most pane lists all of the packages that contain test classes (i.e., subclasses of TestCase). When some of these packages are selected, the test classes that they contain appear in the pane to the right. Abstract classes are italicized, and the test class hierarchy is shown by indentation, so subclasses of ClassTestCase are indented more than subclasses of TestCase. ClassTestCase is a class offering utilities methods to compute test coverage.

Open a Test Runner, select the package *MySetTest*, and click the Run Selected button.

Step 6: Alternative ways to execute tests

You can also run a single test (and print the usual pass/fail result summary) by executing a *Print it* on the following code: `MyExampleSetTest run: #testRemove`.

Some people include an executable comment in their test methods as in `testRemove` below. For example the contents of the comment `self run: #testRemove` can be executed: select the expression inside the comment (but not the comment) and bring the menu to do a *Do it*. It will execute the test.

```
MyExampleSetTest >> testRemove
  "self run: #testRemove"
  | empty full |
  empty := Set new.
  full := Set with: 5 with: 6.
  full remove: 5.
  self assert: (full includes: 6).
  self deny: (full includes: 5)
```

Step 7: Looking at a bug

Introduce a bug in `MyExampleSetTest >> testRemove` and run the tests again. For example, change 6 to 7, as in:

```
MyExampleSetTest >> testRemove
  | empty full |
  empty := Set new.
  full := Set with: 5 with: 6.
  full remove: 5.
  self assert: (full includes: 7).
  self deny: (full includes: 5)
```

The tests that did not pass (if any) are listed in the right-hand panes of the *Test Runner*. If you want to debug one, to see why it failed, just click on the name. Alternatively, you can execute one of the following expressions:

```
(MyExampleSetTest selector: #testRemove) debug

MyExampleSetTest debug: #testRemove
```

Step 8: Interpret the results

The method `assert:` is defined in the class `TestAsserter`. This is a super-class of `TestCase` and therefore all other `TestCase` subclasses and is responsible for all kinds of test result assertions. The `assert:` method expects a boolean argument, usually the value of a tested expression. When the argument is true, the test passes; when the argument is false, the test fails.

There are actually three possible outcomes of a test: *passing*, *failing*, and *raising an error*.

- **Passing**. The outcome that we hope for is that all of the assertions in the test are true, in which case the test passes. In the test runner, when all of the tests pass, the bar at the top turns green.

- **Failing**. The obvious way is that one of the assertions can be false, causing the test to *fail*.

- **Error**. The other possibility is that some kind of error occurs during the execution of the test, such as a *message not understood* error or an *index out of bounds* error. If an error occurs, the assertions in the test method may not have been executed at all, so we can't say that the test has failed; nevertheless, something is clearly wrong!

In the *test runner*, failing tests cause the bar at the top to turn yellow, and are listed in the middle pane on the right, whereas tests with errors cause the bar to turn red, and are listed in the bottom pane on the right.

As an exercise, modify your tests to provoke both errors and failures.

6.6 The SUnit cookbook

This section will give you more details on how to use SUnit. If you have used another testing framework such as JUnit, much of this will be familiar, since all these frameworks have their roots in SUnit. Normally you will use SUnit's GUI to run tests, but there are situations where you may not want to use it.

About assert:equals:

Note that we either used both `assert: aBoolean` and `assert: expression equals: aValue`. The second one provides nicer feedback when the assertion fails. The two following lines are equals.

```
self assert: (empty occurrencesOf: 0) equals: 0.
self assert: (empty occurrencesOf: 0) = 0.
```

Using `assert:equals:` provides a better feedback when the test is failing because we said explicitly that the result should be 0.

Other assertions

In addition to `assert:` and `deny:`, there are several other methods that can be used to make assertions.

First, `assert:description:` and `deny:description:` take a second argument which is a message string that describes the reason for the failure, if it is not obvious from the test itself.

Next, SUnit provides two additional methods, `should:raise:` and `shouldnt:raise:` for testing exception propagation.

For example, you would use `self should: aBlock raise: anException` to test that a particular exception is raised during the execution of `aBlock`. The method below illustrates the use of `should:raise:`.

```
MyExampleSetTest >> testIllegal
  | empty |
  self should: [ empty at: 5 ] raise: Error.
  self should: [ empty at: 5 put: #zork ] raise: Error
```

Try running this test. Note that the first argument of the `should:` and `shouldnt:` methods is a block that contains the expression to be executed.

Running a single test

Normally, you will run your tests using the Test Runner or using your code browser. If you don't want to launch the Test Runner from the World menu, you can execute `TestRunner open`. You can also run a single test as follows:

```
MyExampleSetTest run: #testRemove
>>> 1 run, 1 passed, 0 failed, 0 errors
```

Running all the tests in a test class

Any subclass of `TestCase` responds to the message `suite` and builds a test suite that contains all the methods whose names start with the string *test*.

To run the tests in the suite, send it the message `run`. For example:

```
MyExampleSetTest suite run
>>> 5 run, 5 passed, 0 failed, 0 errors
```

Must I subclass TestCase?

In JUnit you can build a TestSuite from an arbitrary class containing `test*` methods. In SUnit you can do the same but you will then have to create a suite by hand and your class will have to implement all the essential `TestCase` methods like `assert:`. We recommend, however, that you not try to do this. The framework is there: use it.

6.7 Defining a fixture

In the previous example, we defined the context in each test methods and it was a bit boring to duplicate all the logic in any tests. In fact SUnit proposes a solution to this.

Step 1: Define the class and context

We can define the context using the two instance variables `full` and `empty` that we will use to represent a full and an empty set.

```
TestCase subclass: #MyExampleSetTest
  instanceVariableNames: 'full empty'
  classVariableNames: ''
  package: 'MySetTest'
```

Step 2: Setting a reusable context

The method `TestCase >> setUp` defines the context in which each of the tests will run. The message `setUp` is sent before the execution of each test method defined in the test class.

Define the `setUp` method as follows, to initialize the `empty` variable to refer to an empty set and the `full` variable to refer to a set containing two elements.

```
MyExampleSetTest >> setUp
  empty := Set new.
  full := Set with: 5 with: 6
```

In testing jargon the context is called the *fixture* for the test.

Step 3: Write some test methods

Now the previous tests methods are much more compact and contain less duplication.

```
MyExampleSetTest >> testIncludes
  self assert: (full includes: 5).
  self assert: (full includes: 6)
```

```
MyExampleSetTest >> testOccurrences
  self assert: (empty occurrencesOf: 0) equals: 0.
  self assert: (full occurrencesOf: 5) equals: 1.
  full add: 5.
  self assert: (full occurrencesOf: 5) equals: 1
```

```
MyExampleSetTest >> testRemove
  full remove: 5.
  self assert: (full includes: 6).
  self deny: (full includes: 5)
```

6.8   Chapter summary

This chapter explained why tests are an important investment in the future of your code. We explained in a step-by-step fashion how to define a few tests for the class Set.

- To maximize their potential, unit tests should be fast, repeatable, independent of any direct human interaction and cover a single unit of functionality.

- Tests for a class called MyClass belong in a class named MyClassTest, which should be introduced as a subclass of TestCase.

- Initialize your test data in a setUp method.

- Each test method should start with the word *test*.

- Use the TestCase methods assert:, deny: and others to make assertions.

- Run tests!

As exercise, turn the examples given in the first chapter into tests.

CHAPTER **7**

Some collection katas with words

This chapter proposes some little challenges around words and sentences as a way to explore Pharo collections.

7.1 Isogram

An isogram is a word or phrase without a repeating letter. The following words are examples of isograms in english and french:

- egoism, sea, lumberjacks, background, hacking, pathfinder, pharo
- antipode, altruisme, absolument, bigornaux

Isograms are interesting words also because they are often the basis of simple cifers. Isograms of length 10 are commonly used to encode numbers. This way salespeople of products can get access to the original cost of the product and control their sale.

Using the *pathfinder* cipher we can decide that *p* represents the number 1, *a* represents the number 2 and so on. The price tag for an item selling for 1100 Euros may also bear the cryptic letters *frr* written on the back or bottom of the tag. A salesman familiar with the pathfinder cipher will know that the original cost of the item is 500 Euros and he can control his sale.

Since we will essentially manipulate strings, let us start with some basic knowledge on strings.

7.2 About strings

A string in Pharo is in fact an array of characters. We can access string elements using the message at: anIndex. Since all collections in Pharo have their first elements at index 1, the message at: 1 returns the first element of a string.

```
'coucou' at: 1
>>> $c
```

```
'coucou'at: 3
>>> $u
```

As with any collection, we can apply iterators such select:, do:, or collect:. Here we select all the characters that are after, hence bigger, than character $m.

```
'coucou' select: [ :aChar | aChar > $m ]
>>>'ouou'
```

We can also apply all kinds of operations on the collection. Here we reverse it.

```
'coucou' reverse
>>> 'uocuoc'
```

We can also find the index of a string inside another one using the message findString: aString startingAt: anIndex.

```
'coucou' findString: 'ou' startingAt: 1
>>> 2
```

```
'coucou' findString: 'ou' startingAt: 3
>>> 5
```

We simply present some of the possible messages that can be sent to a string. We select some that you can use in the following or in the next chapter. Now let us solve our problem to identify if a string is an isogram.

7.3 A solution using sets

We can do a simple (and not really efficient) implementation using sets. Sets are collections that only contain one occurence of each element added to them. Adding twice the same element only adds one.

Note that sets in Pharo can contain any objects, even sets themselves. This is not the case in all languages. In Pharo, there is no restriction about set elements.

You can convert a string into a set of characters sending the string the message asSet.

```
'coucou' asSet
>>> a Set($u $c $o)
```

Now this is your turn: Imagine how using a set of characters, you can determine if a string is a isogram.

Hints

If the size of a set with the contents of a string and this string are the same, it means that the string does not contain any letter twice! Bingo we can simply identify an isogram.

To get the size of a collection use the message size

```
'coucou' size
>>> 6
```

Now we convert 'coucou' into a set using the message asSet.

```
'coucou' asSet size
>>> 3
```

Note that the message asSet is equivalent to the following script:

```
| s1 |
s1 := Set new.
'coucou' do: [ :aChar | s1 add: aChar ].
s1
>>> a Set($u $c $o)
```

- Here we define a variable s1

- We iterate over all the characters of the string 'coucou', and we add each character one by one to the set s1.

- We return the set.

- The set contains only three elements $c, $o, $u as expected.

Checking expression

So now we can get to the expression that verifies that 'pharo' is an isogram.

```
| s |
s := 'pharo'.
s size = s asSet size
>>> true
```

And that 'phaoro' is not!

```
| s |
s := 'phaoro'.
s size = s asSet size
>>> false
```

Adding a method to the class String

Now we can define a new method to the class String. Since you may propose
multiple implementations, we postfix the message with the implementation
strategy we use. Here we define isIsogramSet

```
String >> isIsogramSet
  "Returns true if the receiver is an isogram, i.e., a word using no
    repetitive character."
  "'pharo' isIsogramSet
  >>> true"
  "'phaoro' isIsogramSet
  >>> false"

  ... Your solution here ...
```

And we test that our method is correct.

```
'pharo' isIsogramSet
>>> true
```

```
'phaoro' isIsogramSet
>>> false
```

Wait! We do not want to have to check manually all the time!

☕ When you verify two times the same things, better write a test! Remember you
write a test once and execute it million times!

7.4 Defining a test

To define tests we could have extended the StringTest class, but we prefer
to define a little class for our own experiment. This way we will create also
a package and move the methods we define as class extension to the that
package.

Important To define a method as a class extension of package Foo, just
name the protocol of the method *Foo.

We define the class GramCheckerTest as follow. It inherits from TestCase
and belong to the package LoopStarGram.

```
TestCase subclass: #GramCheckerTest
  instanceVariableNames: ''
  classVariableNames: ''
  package: 'LoopStarGram'
```

Now we are ready to implement our first automated test for this chapter.

Test methods are special.

- A test method should start with 'test'.

- A test method is executed automatically when we press the icons displaying the method.

- A test method can contain expressions such as self assert: aTrue-Expression or self deny: aFalseExpression.

Here

- Our method is named testIsogramSetImplementation.

- We check (assert:) that 'pharo' is an isogram i.e., that 'pharo' isIsogramSet returns true.

- We check (deny:) that 'phaoro' is *not* an isogram i.e., that 'pharo' isIsogramSet returns false.

```
GramCheckerTest >> testIsogramSetImplementation

  self assert: 'pharo' isIsogramSet.
  self deny: 'phaoro' isIsogramSet.
```

> **Important**   When you write a test, make sure that you test different situations or results. Why? Because imagine that your methods always return true, you would never be sure that not all the string are isograms. So always check for positive and negative results.

Messages assert: and deny: are equivalent as follows: assert (something) is equals to deny(something not) and assert (something not) is equivalent to deny (something). Hence the following expressions are strictly equivalent.

```
  self assert: 'phaoro' isIsogramSet not.
  self deny: 'phaoro' isIsogramSet.
```

Testing several strings

Now we do not want to write a test per string. We want to test multiple strings at the same time. For that we will define a method in the test class that returns a collection of strings. Here we create a methods returning an array of isograms.

```
GramCheckerTest >> isograms
  ^ #('pharo' 'pathfinder' 'xavier' 'francois' 'lumberjacks'
    'altruisme' 'antipode')
```

Then we define a new test method `testAllIsogramSet` that simply iterates over the string array and for each verifies using `assert:` that the element is indeed an isogram.

In Pharo, there are multiple ways to express loops on collection, the easiest is to send the message `do:` to the collection. The `do:` message executes the block to each element of the collection one by one.

The `do:` message executes its argument taking each elements of the receiver collection one by one. Note the way we express it, we ask the collection to iterate on itself. Note also that we do not have to worry about the size of the collection and the index of an element as this is often the case in other languages.

```
GramCheckerTest >> testAllIsogramSet

  self isograms do: [ :word |
    self assert: word isIsogramSet ]
```

Since we said that we should also tests negative let us to the same for non isograms. We create another method that returns non isogram strings and we enhance our testing method.

```
GramCheckerTest >> notIsograms
  ^ #('phaoro' 'stephane' 'idiot' 'freedom')
```

And we make our test using both.

```
GramCheckerTest >> testAllIsogramSetImplementation

  self isograms do: [ :word |
    self assert: word isIsogramSet ].
  self notIsograms do: [ :word |
    self deny: word isIsogramSet ]
```

7.5 Some fun: Obtaining french isograms

Now we would like to find some isograms in french. We stored on the github repository of this book some resources as shown below containing french words line by line. We would like to get all the lines. We will use `ZnClient`, the HTTPClient that comes with Pharo. Since this is a lot of data, execute the expression using the **Inspect It** menu or shortcut to get an inspector instead of a simple **Do It**. You can try the other file which contains more than 330 000 french words.

```
(ZnClient new
    get: 'https://raw.githubusercontent.com/SquareBracketAssociates/
  LearningOOPWithPharo/
  master/resources/listeDeMotsAFrancaisUTF8.txt') lines

(ZnClient new
    get: 'https://raw.githubusercontent.com/SquareBracketAssociates/
  LearningOOPWithPharo/
  master/resources/listeDeMotsFrancaisFrGutUTF8.txt') lines
```

The expression above will give you an array of 336531 words (it is a bit slow depending on your internet connection because it is lot of data).

Once you get the inspector opened, you can start to play with the data. Make sure that you select self and in the text pane you can execute the following expressions:

The first one will select all the words that are isogram and you will see them in the second list that will appear on the right.

```
self select: #isIsogramSet
```

Now you can select again all the isogram longer or equal to 10.

```
self select: [:each | each size >= 10 ]
```

We have other ways to implement isograms and we will discuss such implementations in the next chapter. Now we will play with pangrams.

7.6 Pangrams

The definition of a pangram is the following: *A Pangram or holoalphabetic sentence for a given alphabet is a sentence using every letter of the alphabet at least once.*

Here are examples of english pangrams:

- the five boxing wizards jump quickly
- the quick brown fox jumps over the lazy dog

Let us write a test first. Yes we want to make sure that we will be able to control if our code is correct and we do not want to repeat typing the test.

```
GramCheckerTest >> testIsEnglishPangram

  self assert: 'The quick brown fox jumps over the lazy dog'
    isEnglishPangram.
  self deny: 'The quick brown fox jumps over the  dog'
    isEnglishPangram
```

Imagine a solution

Imagine that we have a collection or string representing the alphabet. A solution is to check that the potential pangram string contains each of the characters of the alphabet, as soon as we see that one character is missing we stop and know that the sentence is not a pangram.

```
'The quick brown fox jumps over the lazy dog' isEnglishPangram
>>> true
'The quick brown fox jumps over the dog' isEnglishPangram
>>> false
```

A first version

Here is a first version. We define a variable isPangram that will represent the information we know about the receiver. We set it to true to start. Then we iterate over an alphabet character by character and as soon as the character is not included in the receiver we set the variable to false. At the end we return the variable isPangram.

```
String >> isEnglishPangram
  "Returns true is the receiver is a pangram i.e., that it uses all
    the characters of a given alphabet."

  | isPangram |
  isPangram := true.
  'abcdefghijklmnopqrstuvwxyz' do: [ :aChar |
    (self includes: aChar)
      ifFalse: [ isPangram := false ]
    ].
  ^ isPangram
```

This first implementation has a problem. Can you see which one? If the sentence does not contain $a, we will know it immediately still we will look for all the other letters. So this is clearly inefficient.

A better version

Instead for testing all characters, even if we know one is missing, what we should do is to stop looking as soon as we identify that there is one missing character and return the result.

The following definition is doing this and it deserves a word of explanation.

The expression ^ something returns the value something to the caller method. The program execution exits at that point: it does not execute the rest of method. The program execution returns to the method caller. Usually we use ^ something as last statement of a method when they need to return a special value. Now ^ anExpression can occur anywhere and in particular inside a loop. In such a case the loop is stopped, the method execution is stopped and the value is returned.

```
String >> isEnglishPangram
  "Returns true is the receiver is a pangram i.e., that it uses all
    the characters of a given alphabet."

  'abcdefghijklmnopqrstuvwxyz' do: [ :aChar |
    (self includes: aChar)
      ifFalse: [ ^ false ]
  ].
  ^ true
```

Note that we do not need the variable isPangram anymore. We return true as last expression because we assume that if the execution arrives to the this point, it means that all the characters of the alphabet are in the receiver, else the execution would have been stopped and false would have been returned.

When you define a method returning a boolean value, always think that you should at least return a true and a false value. This sounds like a stupid advice but developing such a basic reflex is important.

> **Important**   The execution of any expression preceded by a ^ (a caret) will cause the method to exit at that point, returning the value of that expression. A method that terminates without explicitly returning some expression will implicitly return self.

7.7   Handling alphabet

A pangram is only valid within a given alphabet. The web site http://clagnut. com/blog/2380/ describes pangrams in many different languages. Now we could follow one gag in Gaston Lagaffe with the 'Il y a des poux. Parmi les poux, il y a des poux papas et des poux pas papas. Parmi les poux papas, il y a des poux papas papas et des poux papas non papas....' and all their descendance. 'les poux papas et les poux pas papas' is not a pangram in french but a pangram in the alphabet 'apouxetl'.

We would like to be able to specify the alphabet to be used to verify. Yes we define a new test.

```
GramCheckerTest >> testIsPangramIn

  self assert: ('The quick brown fox jumps over the lazy dog'
    isPangramIn: 'abcdefghijklmnopqrstuvwxyz').
  self assert: ('les poux papas et les poux pas papas' isPangramIn:
    'apouxetl').
```

You can do it really simply:

```
String >> isPangramIn: alphabet
  "Returns true is the receiver is a pangram i.e., that it uses all
    the characters of a given alphabet."
  "'The quick brown fox jumps over the lazy dog' isPangramIn:
    'abcdefghijklmnopqrstuvwxyz'
  >>> true"
  "'tata' isPangramIn: 'at'
  >>> true"

  ... Your solution ...
```

```
String >> isEnglishPangram
  "Returns true is the receiver is a pangram i.e., that it uses all
    the characters of a given alphabet."
  "'The quick brown fox jumps over the lazy dog' isEnglishPangram
  >>> true"
  "'The quick brown fox jumps over the dog' isEnglishPangram
  >>> false"

  ... Your solution ...
```

Execute all the tests to verify that we did not change anything.

If we keep to use french words that do not need accents, we can verify that some french sentences are also pangrams.

```
'portez ce vieux whisky au juge blond qui fume' isEnglishPangram
>>> true

'portons dix bons whiskys à l''avocat goujat qui fume au zoo.'
    isEnglishPangram
>>> true
```

7.8 Identifying missing letters

Building a pangram can be difficult and the question is how we can identify missing letters. Let us define some methods to help us. But first let us write a test.

We will start to write a test for the method detectFirstMissingLetter-For:. As you see we just remove one unique letter from our previous pangram and we are set.

```
GramCheckerTest >> testDetectFirstMissingLetter

  self assert: ('the quick brown fox jumps over the lzy dog'
    detectFirstMissingLetterFor: 'abcdefghijklmnopqrstuvwxyz')
    equals: $a.
  self assert: ('the uick brown fox jumps over the lazy dog'
    detectFirstMissingLetterFor: 'abcdefghijklmnopqrstuvwxyz')
```

```
      equals: $q.
```

Your work: Propose a definition for the method `detectFirstMissingLet-terFor:`.

```
String >> detectFirstMissingLetterFor: alphabet
  "Return the first missing letter to make a pangram of the receiver
    in the context of a given alphabet.
  Return '' otherwise"

  ... Your solution ...
```

In fact this method is close to the method `isPangramIn: alphabet`. It should iterate over the alphabet and check that the char is included in the string. When this is not the case, it should return the character and we can return an empty string when there is no missing letter.

About the return values of detectFirstMissingLetterFor:

Returning objects that are not polymorphic such as a single character or a string (which is not a character but a sequence of characters) is really bad design. Why? Because the user of the method will be forced to check if the result is a single character or a collection of characters.

Avoid as much as possible to return objects that are not polymorphic. Return a collection and an empty collection. Not a collection and nil. Write methods returning the same kind of objects, this way their clients will be able to treat them without asking if they are different. This practice reinforces the **Tell do not ask principle**.

We have two choices: either always return a collection as for that we convert the character into a string sending it the message `asString` as follow, or we can return a special character to represent that nothing happens for example Character space.

```
String >> detectFirstMissingLetterFor: alphabet
  "Return the first missing letter to make a pangram of the receiver
    in the context of a given alphabet.
  Return '' otherwise"

  alphabet do: [ :aChar |
    (self includes: aChar)
      ifFalse: [ ^ aChar asString ]
    ].
  ^ ''
```

Here we prefer to return a string since the method is returning the first character. In the following one we return a special character.

```
String >> detectFirstMissingLetterFor: alphabet
  "Return the first missing letter to make a pangram of the receiver
    in the context of a given alphabet.
  Return '' otherwise"

  alphabet do: [ :aChar |
    (self includes: aChar)
      ifFalse: [ ^ aChar ]
    ].
  ^ Character space
```

Now it is better to return all the missing letters.

Detecting all the missing letters

Let us write a test to cover this new behavior. We removed the character a and g from the pangram and we verify that the method returns an array with the corresponding missing letters.

```
GramCheckerTest >> testDetectAllMissingLetters

  self assert: ('the quick brown fox jumps over the lzy do'
    detectAllMissingLettersFor: 'abcdefghijklmnopqrstuvwxyz')
    equals: #($a $g).
  self assert: ('the uick brwn fx jumps ver the lazy dg'
    detectAllMissingLettersFor: 'abcdefghijklmnopqrstuvwxyz')
    equals: #($q $o).
```

Your work: Implement the method detectAllMissingLettersFor:.

```
String >> detectAllMissingLettersFor: alphabet

  ... Your solution ...
```

One of the problem that you can encounter is that the order of the missing letters can make the tests failed. You can create a Set instead of an Array.

Now our test does not work because it verifies that we get an array of characters while we get an ordered collection. So we change it to take into account the returned collection.

```
GramCheckerTest >> testDetectAllMissingLetters

  self assert: ('the quick brown fox jumps over the lzy do'
    detectAllMissingLettersFor: 'abcdefghijklmnopqrstuvwxyz')
    equals: (Set withAll: #($a $g)).
  self assert: ('the uick brwn fx jumps ver the lazy dg'
    detectAllMissingLettersFor: 'abcdefghijklmnopqrstuvwxyz')
    equals: #($q $o) asSet.
```

Instead of explicitly creating a Set, we could also use the message asSet that converts the receiver into a Set as shown in the second check.

7.9 **Palindrome as exercise**

We let as an exercise the identification if a string is a palindrom. A palindrome is a word or sentence that can be read in both way. 'KAYAK' is a palindrome.

```
GramCheckerTest >> testIsPalindrome

    self assert: 'ete' isPalindrome.
    self assert: 'kayak' isPalindrome.
    self deny: 'etat' isPalindrome.
```

Some possible implementations

Here is a list of possible implementation.

- You can iterate on strings and check that the first element and the last element are the same.

- You can also reverse the receiver (message reverse) and compare the character one by one. You can use the message with:do: which iterate on two collections.

```
'etat' reverse
>>> 'tate'
```

```
| res |
res := OrderedCollection new.
#(1 2 3) with: #(10 20 30) do: [ :f :s | res add: f * s ].
res
>>> an OrderedCollection(10 40 90)
```

You can also add the fact that space do not count.

```
    self assert: 'Elu par cette crapule' isPalindrome.
```

7.10 **Conclusion**

We got some fun around words and sentences. You should know more about strings and collection. In particular, in Pharo a collection can contain any objects. You also saw is that loops to not require to specify the first index and how to increment it. Of course we can do it in Pharo using the message to:do: and to:by:do:. But only when we need it. So play with some iterators such as do: and select:. The iterators are really powerful and this is really important to be fluent with them because they will make you save a lot of time.

Part II

About objects and classes

In this part of the book we suggest carefully reading the first chapter before continuing with the rest. The other chapters contain extremely simple exercises which may be tedious to read in one sitting.

CHAPTER 8

Objects and classes

Pharo is a pure object-oriented programming language, i.e., everything in the system is an object i.e., an entity created by a class and reacting to messages.

This chapter presents key mechanisms that characterize object-oriented programming: *objects*, *classes*, *messages* and *methods*. We will also present *distribution of responsibilities* which is one of the heart of object-oriented programming as well as *delegation* and *composition*. Each of these mechanisms will be used and illustrated again in this book.

We start explaining objects, classes, messages and methods with really simple examples. Then in the following chapter we will propose an example that illustrates what we can achieve by using objects of different classes.

Objects are created by *classes* that are object factories: Classes define the structure and behavior of objects (in terms of methods) but each object has a specific state and identity that is unique and different from all other objects. A class defines *methods* that specify how a *message* is actually implemented.

8.1 Objects: Entities reacting to messages

Instead of a bit-grinding processor ... plundering data structures, we have a universe of well-behaved objects that courteously ask each other to carry out their various desires. [Ingall 81]

Object-oriented programming is about creating objects and interacting with objects by sending them *messages*.

Objects are entities that communicate via messages and react to messages by executing certain tasks. Moreover objects hide the way they define these tasks: the client of an object send a message to an object and the system find the corresponding method to be executed. Messages specify what should be done and methods how it should be done.

Turtles as an example

Imagine that we have a graphics turtle like a LOGO turtle. We do the following: create a turtle, send it messages to make it move, turn, and trace some drawings. Let us look at this in detail.

Creating an object

First we create a new turtle by sending the message new to the class Turtle.

```
| t |
t := Turtle new.
```

A class is a cast for objects. All the objects, instances of a class, share the same characteristics and behavior. For example, all the turtle instances have a direction and understand messages to rotate and move. However, each turtle has its own value for its direction. We say that all the instances of a class have the same instance variables but each as private value for them.

Sending messages

The only way to interact with objects is to send them *messages*. In the following snippets we send messages

- to create an object , message new,
- to tell the turtle to turn, message turn:, and
- to tell the turtle to move, message go:.

```
| t |
t := Turtle new.
t turn: 90.
t go: 100.
t turn: 180.
t go: 100.
```

When an object receives a message, it reacts by performing some actions. An object can return a value, change its internal state, or send messages to other objects. Here the turtle will change its direction and it will interact with the display to leave a trail.

Multiple instances: each with its own state.

We can have multiple objects of the same class and each one has a specific state. Here we have two turles each one located to a specific position and pointing into its own direction.

```
| t1 t2 |
t1 := Turtle new.
t1 turn: 90.
t1 go: 100.
t1 turn: 180.
t1 go: 100.
t2 := Turtle new.
t2 go: 100.
t2 turn: 40.
t2 go: 100.
```

8.2   Messages and Methods

Messages specify *what* the object should do and not how it should do it (this is the duties of methods). When we send the message go: we just specify what we expect the receiver to do. Sending a message is similar to the abstraction provided by procedures or functions in procedural or functional programming language: it hides implementation details. However sending a message is much more than executing a sequence of instructions: it means that we have to find the method that should be executed in reaction to the message.

Message: what should be executed

The message square: is send to a new turtle with 100 as argument. The message expresses what the receiver should do.

```
Turtle new square: 100
```

Method: how we execute it

The method definition square: below defines step by step what are the actions to be done in response to the message square:. It defines that to draw a square the turtle receiving the message square: (represented by self) should perform four times the following sequences of messages: move forward a distance (message go:), turn 90 degrees (using the message turn:).

```
square: size
   4 timesRepeat: [ self go: size; turn: 90 ]
```

Note that finding the method corresponding to the message is done at runtime and depends on the object receiving the message.

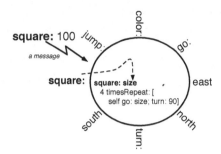

Figure 8-1 An object presents to the other objects an interface composed of a set of messages defining *what* he can do. This behavior is realized by methods that specify *how* the behavior is implemented. When a message is sent to an object a method with the message name (called selector) is looked up and executed.

💻 A message represents *what* the object should do, while a method specifies *how* the behavior is realized.

An object can also send messages to other objects. For example, when a turtle draws a line, it sends messages to an object representing the line color and its length.

💻 An object is an entity that once created receives messages and performs some actions in reaction. When a message is sent to an object, a method with the message name is looked up and executed.

8.3 An object is a protective entity

An object is responsible of the way it realizes its reaction to a message. It *offers services* but *hides* the way they are implemented (see Figure 8-2). We do not have to know how the method associated with the message selector is implemented. Only the object knows the exact definition of the method. This is when we define the method square: that defines how a turtle draws a square of a given size, that we focus on *how* a turtle draws a square. Figure 8-2 shows the message and the method square:. The method square: defines how to draw step by step a square, however the object only offers the message square: and does not show it implementation.

> **Important**   An object presents to the other objects an *interface* (i.e., a set of messages) defining *what* the object can do. This behavior is realized by methods that specify *how* the behavior is implemented. To perform something useful some data are most of the time required. Data are only accessed by the methods.

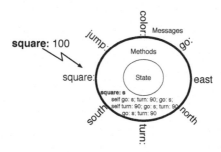

Figure 8-2   The message square: can be implemented differently. This different implementation does not impact the sender of the message who is not concerned by the internals of the object.

From a turtle *user* point of view, the only relevant information is that the turtle effectively receiving the message square: executes the method that draws a square. So changing the definition of the square: method to the one below does not have any consequence on the methods that call it. Figure 8-2 illustrates this point.

```
square: s
    "Make the receiver draw a square of size s"

    self go: s; turn: 90; go: s; turn: 90.
    self go: s; turn: 90; go: s; turn: 90
```

Hiding the internal representation is not limited to object-oriented programming but it is central to object-oriented programming.

> **Important**   An object is responsible of the way it realizes its reaction to a message. It offers services and hides the way they are implemented.

8.4   An object protects its data

An object holds some *private data* that represents its state (see Figure 8-3). Moreover, it controls its state and should not let other objects play directly with them because this could let him into an inconsistent state. For example, you do not want to somebody else plays with the data of your bank account directly and really want to control your transaction.

For example, a LOGO turtle can be represented by a position, a direction and a way to indicate if its pen is up or down. But, we cannot directly access these data and change them. For that we have to use the set of messages proposed by a turtle. These methods constitute the *interface* of an object. We say that the object state is *encapsulated*, this means that not everybody can access

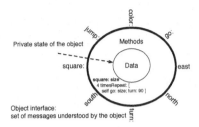

Figure 8-3   A turtle is an object which has an interface, i.e., a set of messages to which it can reply and a private state that only its methods can access.

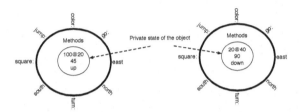

Figure 8-4   Two turtles have the same interface, i.e., set of messages being understood but they have *different* private state representing their direction, position and pen status.

it. In fact, object-oriented programming is based on encapsulation, i.e., the fact that per default objects are the only ones that can access their own state.

In Pharo, a client cannot access the state of an object if the object does not define a method to access it. Moreover, clients should not rely on the internal representation of an object because an object is free to change the way it implements its behavior. Exposing the internal state of an object by defining methods providing access to the object data weakens the control that an object has over its own state.

> **Important**   An object holds some *private* data that represents its *internal* state. Each object has its own state. Two objects of the same class share the same *interface* but have their own private state.

8.5 With counters

Now that you got the main point of objects, we can see that it applies to everything. In Pharo *everything* is an object. In fact there is *nothing* else, only objects. Here is a little program with counters.

We create two counters that we store in variables c1 and c2 instances of the class Counter. Each counter has its own state but exhibits the same behavior as all the counters defined by the class Counter:

- when responding to the message count, it returns its value,
- when responding to the message increment, it increment one to its current value.

```
| c1 c2 |
c1 := Counter new.
c2 := Counter new.
c1 count.
>>> 0
c1 increment.
c1 increment.
c1 count.
>>> 2
c2 count.
>>> 0
c 2 increment.
c2 count.
>>> 1
```

8.6 A class: blueprint or factory of objects

A class is a mold or cast of objects. A class specifies two important aspects of their instances:

- Instance **structure**. All the instances of a class will have the same structure expressed in terms of *instance variables*. Pay attention that the variables are the same for all the instances of a class but not their values. Each instance has specific values for its instance variables.
- Instance **behavior**. All the instances share the same behavior even if this one can be different because applied on different values.

Important   A class is as a blueprint for its instances. It is a factory of objects. All objects will have the same structure and share a common behavior.

Let us illustrate this with the class Counter.

Object structure

Let us study the Counter class definition.

```
Object subclass: #Counter
  instanceVariableNames: 'count'
  classVariableNames: ''
  package: 'LOOP'
```

The expresion `Object subclass: #Counter` indicates that the class `Counter` is a subclass of the class `Object`. It means that counter instances understand the messages defined also by the class `Object`. In Pharo, classes should at least be a subclass of the class `Object`. You will learn more about subclassing and inheritance in Chapter 14.

Then the class `Counter` defines that all the instances will have one instance variable named `count` using the expression `instanceVariableNames: 'count'`. And each instance of the class `Counter` will have a `count` variable with a *different* value as we showed in the examples above.

Finally the class is defined in the package `'LOOP'`. A package is a kind of folder containing multiple classes.

Object behavior

In addition a class is the place that groups the behavior of its instances. Indeed since all the instances of the class share the *same* behavior definitions, such behavior is defined and grouped in a class.

For counters, the class defines how to retrieve the counter value, how to increment and decrement the count as used in the messages in the previous code snippets.

Here is the definition of the **method** `increment`. It simply adds one to the instance variable `count`.

```
Counter >> increment
  count := count + 1
```

When we send a message to a counter for example in the expression `c1 increment`, the method `increment` will be applied on *that* specific object `c1`. In the expression `c1 increment`, `c1` is called the **receiver** of the message `increment`.

In the method `increment`, the variable `count` refers to the variable of the **receiver** of the message.

A class defines methods that specify the behavior of all the instances created by the class.

Multiple methods can accessed to the instance variables of the receiver. For example the methods `increment`, `count: decrement` and `printOn:` all access the instance variable `count` of the receiver to perform different computation.

```
Counter >> count: anInteger
    count := anInteger
```

```
Counter >> decrement
    count := count - 1
```

```
Counter >> printOn: aStream
    super printOn: aStream.
    aStream nextPutAll: ' with value: ', self count printString.
```

For example, once the following program is executed the count instance variable of the counter c2 will hold the value 11, since the method count: will set its value to 10, and increment will set it to 11 and 12 and finally decrement will set it to 11.

```
| c2 |
c2 := Counter new.
c2 count: 10.
c2 increment.
c2 increment.
c2 decrement.
```

Self is the message receiver

Imagine that now we would like to send a message to the object that receives the message itself. We need a way to refer to this object. Pharo defines a special variable for this exact purpose: self.

Important   self always refers to the message receiver that is currently executed.

For example we can implement the method incrementByTwo as follows:

```
Counter >> incrementByTwo
    self increment.
    self increment
```

When we execute the expression c1 incrementByTwo, during the execution of the method incrementByTwo, self refers to c1.

We will explain how a method is found when a message is sent but first we should explain inheritance, i.e., how a class is defined incrementally from a root class and all this will be explained in Chapter 14.

8.7   Class and instances are really different

Classes and objects are different objects; they understand different messages.

For example, sending new to the Counter class returns a newly created counter, while sending new to a counter results in an error. In the opposite way, sending increment to the class Counter leads also to an error because the class Counter is a factory of objects not the objects themselves.

A class is a factory of objects. A class creates instances. An instance does not create other instances of the class.

☕ A class describes the structure (instance variables) and the behavior (methods) of *all* its instances. The state of an instance is the value of its instance variables and it is specific to one single object while the behavior is shared by all the instances of a class.

8.8 Conclusion

In this chapter you saw that:

- An object is a computer entity that once created receives messages and performs some actions in reaction.

- An object has an unique identity.

- An object holds some private data that represent its internal state.

- A class is a factory of objects: It *describes* the internal structure of all its instances by means of instance variable.

- All objects of the same class share the same behavior, i.e., the same method definitions.

- Instance variables are accessible by all the methods of a class. Instance variables have the same lifetime than the object to which they belong to.

- In Pharo , instance variables cannot be accessed from outside of an object. Instance variables are only accessible from the methods of the class that define them.

- Methods define the behavior of all the instances of the class they belong to.

CHAPTER **9**

Revisiting objects and classes

In the previous chapter we presented objects and classes via simple examples. In this chapter we introduce a little bit more elaborated example: a little file system where we revisit everything and extend it to explain *late binding, distribution of responsibilities* and *delegation.* The file example will be extended to present *inheritance* in Chapter 14.

9.1 A simple and naive file system

We start to present a simple example that we use to present and explain the concepts: a simple and naive file system as shown in Figure 9-1. What the diagram shows is that we have:

- files that also have a name and a contents. Here we get three different files Babar, Astroboy and tintinEtLesPicaros.

- directories that have a name and can contain other files or directories. Here we get the manga, comics, oldcomics and belgiumSchool directories. Directories can be nested: comics contains three repositories. The belgiumSchool directory contains tintinEtLesPicaros.

Figure 9-1 Some directories and files organised in a file system.

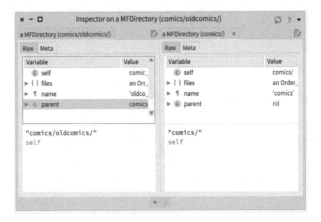

Figure 9-2 Inspecting dOldComics and clicking on the parent variable.

9.2 Studying a first scenario

Since what we want to develop may be a bit unclear for us, let us define first an example. In the rest of this book we will code such examples as tests that can automatically be executed. For now it would make the discourse too complex, so we just use little code examples.

We create two directories.

```
| dComics dOldComics dManga |
dComics := MFDirectory new name: 'comics'.
dOldComics := MFDirectory new name: 'oldcomics'.
```

We add the oldcomics folder to comics and we check that the parent children relationship is well set.

```
...
dComics addElement: dOldComics.
dOldComics parent == dComics
>>> true
```

Here we verify that the parent of dOldComics is dComics: the message `==` checks that the receiver is the same object than the argument.

You can also inspect the receiver as follows and if you click on the instance variable parent of the receiver you should obtain the situation depicted by Figure 9-2.

```
...
dOldComics inspect
```

We continue with some queries.

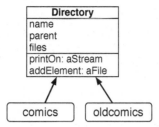

Figure 9-3   The Directory class and some instances (directories).

```
   ...
dComics parent
>>> nil
```

Here we verify that dOldComics is comprised in the children of dComics.

```
   ...
dComics children includes: dOldComics.
>>> true
```

We create a new repository and we check that once added to a parent repository, it is included in the children.

```
dManga := MFDirectory new name: 'manga'.
dComics addElement: dManga.
dComics children includes: dManga
>>> true
```

9.3   Defining a class

Let us start by defining the directory class.

```
Object subclass: #MFDirectory
   instanceVariableNames: 'parent name files'
   classVariableNames: ''
   package: 'MyFS'
```

When we create a directory, its files is an empty ordered collection. This is what we express in the following method initialize.

```
MFDirectory >> initialize
   files := OrderedCollection new
```

A newly created object is sent the message initialize just after its creation. Therefore the initialize method is executed.

Now we can write the method addElement:. (To keep things simple, note that we consider that when a file is added to a directory, it was not belonging to a another directory. This behavior could be implemented by aFile moveTo: aDirectory) Adding a file to a directory means: (1) that the parent of the file is changed to be the directory to which it is added, (2) that the added file is added to the list of files contained in the directory.

```
MFDirectory >> addElement: aFile
  aFile parent: self.
  files add: aFile
```

Note that the method name addElement: is not nice but we chose it on purpose so that you do not believe that delegating requires that the methods have the same name. An object can delegate its part of duties to another object by simply passing a message.

We should then define the methods name:, parent:, parent, and children to be able to run our example.

```
MFDirectory >> name: aString
  name := aString
```

```
MFDirectory >> parent: aFile
  parent := aFile
```

```
MFDirectory >> parent
  ^ parent
```

```
MFDirectory >> children
  ^ files
```

With such method definitions, our little example should run. It should not print the same results because we did not change the printing of the objects yet.

A first little analysis

When we look at the implementation of the method to add a file to a directory we see that the class MFDirectory used another class OrderedCollection to store the information about the files it contains. An ordered collection is a quite complex object: it can insert, remove elements, grow its size, and many more operations.

We say that the class MFDirectory delegates a part of its duties (to keep the information of the files it contains) to the class OrderedCollection. In addition, when an object is executed, the object to which it may delegate part of its computation may change dynamically.

Such behavior is not specific to object-oriented programming, in procedural languages we can call another function defined on a data structure. Now with object-oriented programming, there is a really important point: an object will send messages to other objects (even from the same class) and such message send will use the message offered by the receiver. There is normally no way for an object to access the internal structure of another object.

9.4 **Printing a directory**

Now we would like to get the directory printed in a better way. Without too much explanation, you should know that the method printOn: astream of an object is executed when the system or we send the message printString to an object. So we can specialise it.

The argument passed to the method printOn: is a stream. A stream is an object in which we can store information one after the other in sequence using the message <<. The argument of << should be a sequence of objects such as string (which is a sequence of characters).

```
MFDirectory >> printOn: aStream
  aStream << name
```

Let us try.

```
| el1 el2 |
el1 := MFDirectory new name: 'comics'.
el2 := MFDirectory new name: 'oldcomics'.
el1 addElement: el2.
el1 printString
>>> 'comics'
```

```
  ...
el2 printString
>>> 'oldcomics'
```

What would be nice is to get the full path so that we can immediately understand the configuration. For example we would like to finish with a '/' to indicate that this is a directory as with the ls command on unix.

```
| el1 el2 |
el1 := MFDirectory new name: 'comics'.
el2 := MFDirectory new name: 'oldcomics'.
el1 addElement: el2.
el1 >> printString.
>>>'comics'
```

```
  ...
el2 printString
>>> 'comics/oldcomics/'
```

A possible definition is the following one:

```
MFDirectory >> printOn: aStream
  parent isNil
    ifFalse: [ parent printOn: aStream ].
  aStream << name.
  aStream << '/'
```

Try it and it should print the expected results. What do we see with this definition: it is a kind of recursive definition. The name of a directory is in fact

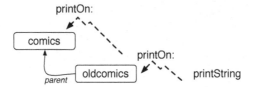

Figure 9-4 Navigating an object graph by sending message to different objects.

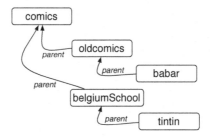

Figure 9-5 A graph of objects to represent our file system.

the concatenation (here we just add in the stream but this is the same.) of the name of its parents (as shown in Figure 9-4). Similar to a recursive function navigating a structure composed of similar elements (like a linked-list or any structure defined by induction), each parent receives and executes another time the `printOn:` method and returns the name for its part.

9.5 Adding files

Now we want to add files. Once we will have defined files we will be able to have a graph of objects of different kinds represent our file system with directories and files as shown in Figure 9-5.

An example first

Again let us start with an example. A file should contain some contents.

```
| el1 dOldComics |
el1 := MFFile new name: 'astroboy'; contents: 'The story of a boy
    turned into a robot that saved the world'.
dOldComics := MFDirectory new name: 'oldcomics'.
dOldComics addElement: el1.
el1 printString.
>>>
'oldcomics/astroboy'
```

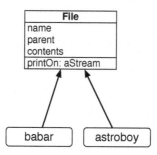

Figure 9-6 A new class and its instances.

A new class definition

Again a file needs a name, a parent and in addition a contents.

We define the class MFFile as follows and illustrated in Figure 9-6. Note that this solution is not satisfactory and we will propose a much better one later.

```
Object subclass: #MFFile
  instanceVariableNames: 'parent name contents'
  classVariableNames: ''
  package: 'MyFS'
```

As for the directories we initialize the contents of a file with a default value.

```
MFFile >> initialize
  contents := ''
```

We should define the same methods for parent:, parent and name:. This duplication coupled with the fact that we get nearly the same class definition should be a clear warning. It means that we do not reuse enough and that if we want to change the system we will have to change it multiple times and we may introduce errors by forgetting one place. We will address it in Chapter 14. In addition we will add a method to be able to set the contents of the file contents:.

```
MFFile >> name: aString
  name := aString
```

```
MFFile >> parent: aFile
  parent := aFile
```

```
MFFile >> parent
  ^ parent
```

```
MFFile >> contents: aString
  contents := aString
```

At the stage we should be able to define a file and adding it to a directory.

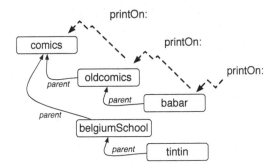

Figure 9-7 Printing a file: Sending messages inside a graph of different objects.

Now we should redefine the implementation of printOn: to print nicely the name of file:

```
MFFile >> printOn: aStream
    aStream << name
```

But this is not enough because we will just get 'astroboy' and not 'old-comics/astroboy'. So let us improve it.

```
MFFile >> printOn: aStream
    parent isNil ifFalse: [
        parent printOn: aStream ].
    aStream << name
```

9.6 One message and multiple methods

Before continuing let us step back and analyse the situation. We send the same messages and we execute different methods.

```
| el1 dOldComics dComics |
el1 := MFFile new name: 'astroboy'; contents: 'The story of a boy
    turned into a robot that saved the world'.
dOldComics := MFDirectory new name: 'oldcomics'.
dComics := MFDirectory new name: 'comics'.
dComics addElement: dOldComics.
dOldComics addElement: el1.
el1 printString.
>>>
'comics/oldcomics/astroboy'
```

```
dOldComics printString.
>>>
'comics/oldcomics/'
```

What we see is that there is one message and several implementations of methods and that sending a message will find and execute the correct method.

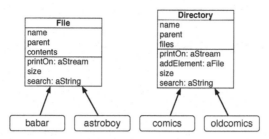

Figure 9-8   Two classes understanding similar sets of message.

For example, there are two methods printOn: one for file and one for directory but only one message printOn: sent from the printString message.

In addition a method can be defined in terms of messages sent to other objects. The method printOn: for directories is complex and it delegates the
same message to other objects, its parents (as illustrated by Figure 9-7). The
method addElement: delegates to the OrderedCollection sending a different
message add:.

9.7   Objects: stepping back

Now that we saw some examples of objects, it is time to step back. Objects
are defined by the values of their state, their behavior (shared with the other
instances of their class) and an identity.

- **State.** Each object has specific values. While all the instances of classes
  have the same structure, each instance has its own values. Each object has a private state. Clients or users of an object cannot access the
  state of the object if this one does not explicitly expose it by defining a
  method returning it (such as the message count).

- **Behavior.** Each object shares the same behavior with all the instances
  of its class.

- **Identity.** An object has an identity. It is unique. oldcomics is clearly
  not the same as comics.

9.8   Examples of distribution of responsibilities

We will now implement two functionalities: the size of directories and a
search based on the contents of the files. This will set the context to explain
the key concept of distribution of responsibilities.

File size

Let us imagine that we want to compute the size of a directory. Note that the size computation we propose is fantasist but this is for the sake of the example. To perform such a computation we should also define what is the size of a file. Again let us start with examples (that you will turn into tests in the future.).

First we define the file size as the size of its name plus the size of its contents.

```
| el |
el := MFFile new name: 'babar'; contents: 'Babar et Celeste'.
el size = 'babar' size + 'Babar et Celeste' size.
>>> true
```

Second we define the directory size as its name size plus the size of its files and we add and arbitrary number: 2.

```
| p2 el |
el := MFFile new name: 'babar'.
p2 := MFDirectory new name: 'oldcomics'.
p2 addElement: el.
p2 size = 'oldcomics' size + 'babar' size + 2
>>> true
```

We define two methods size one for each class (see Figure 9-8).

```
MFFile >> size
    ^ contents size + name size
```

```
MFDirectory >> size
    | sum |
    sum := 0.
    files do: [ :each | sum := sum + each size ].
    sum := sum + name size.
    sum := sum + 2.
    ^ sum
```

Search

Let us imagine that we want to search the files matching a given string. Here is an example to set the stage.

```
| p el1 el2 |
p := MFDirectory new name: 'comics'.
el1 := MFFile new name: 'babar'; contents: 'Babar et Celeste'.
p addElement: el1.
el2 := MFFile new name: 'astroboy'; contents: 'super cool robot'.
p addElement: el2.
(p search: 'Ba') includes: el1
>>> true
```

To implement this behavior is quite simple: we define two methods one in each class (as shown in Figure 9-8).

```
MFFile >> search: aString
   ^ '*', aString, '*' match: contents
```

```
MFDirectory >> search: aString
   ^ files select: [ :eachFile | eachFile search: aString ]
```

9.9   Important points

These two examples show several *important* points:

Modular thinking

Each method is modular in the sense that it only focuses on the behavior of the objects specified by the class defining the method. Such method can be built by sending other messages without having to know how such methods are defined. It also means that we can add a new kind of classes or remove one without having to change the entire system.

Sending a message is making a choice

We send *one* message and one method amongst the *multiple* methods with the same name will be selected and executed. The method is dynamically looked up during execution as we will see in Chapters 14 and 13. Sending a message is selecting the corresponding method having the same name than the message. When a message is sent to an object the corresponding method is looked in the class of the message receiver.

> **Important**   Sending a message is making a choice. The system selects for us the correct method to be executed.

Polymorphic objects

We created objects (files and directories) that are *polymorphic* in the sense that they offer a common set of messages (search:, printOn:, size, parent:). This is really powerful because we can compose objects (for example add a new directory or a file) without changing the program. Imagine that we add a new kind of directories we can introduce it and reuse extending programs based on size or search: *without* changing them.

> **Important**   Creating polymorphic objects is a really powerful capability. It lets us extend and change programs without breaking them.

Most of the time it is better to give similar name to methods performing similar behavior, and different names when the methods are doing semantically different actions, so that users of the objects are not confused.

The polymorphism is really a strength of object-oriented languages because it allows one to treat different objects, i.e., instances of different classes, uniformly as soon as they implement the same messages. Polymorphism works in synergy with the idea that an object is responsible to decide how to react to message reception. Indeed, the fact that different objects can implement the same messages let us write code that only tell the objects to execute some actions without worrying exactly about the kind of objects.

9.10 Distribution of responsibilities

This example as well as the printing of files and directories illustrates something fundamental in object-oriented programming: the distribution of responsibilities. With the distribution of responsibilities, each kind of objects is responsible for a specific behavior and a more elaborated behavior is composed out of such different behavior. The size of a directory is computed based on the size of its files by requesting the files to compute their size.

Procedural

Let us take some time to compare with procedural thinking. Computing the size of a list of files and directories would have been expressed as a monolitic behavior sketch below:

```
sizeOfFiles: files
  | sum |
  sum := 0.
  files do: [ :aFile |
    aFile class = MFFile
      ifTrue: [ sum := sum + aFile name size + aFile contents size ].
    aFile class = MFDirectory
      ifTrue: [
        | fileSum |
        fileSum := 0.
        each files do: [:anInsideFile | fileSum := fileSum +
    anInsideFile name size + anInsideFile contents size ].
        sum := sum + fileSum + each name size + 2].
  ^ sum
```

While this example is a bit exagerated, we see several points:

- First, we explicitly check the kind of structures we are manipulating. If this is a file or directory we do something different.

- Second, the logic of the computation is defined inside the `sizeOf-Files:` itself, and not in the entities themselves. This means in particular that such logic cannot be reused.

- A part of the implementation logic is exposed and not in control of the object. It means that if we decide to change the internal structure of our classes, we will have to change this function too.

- Adding a new kind of such as a root directory is not modular. We will have to modify the method `sizeOfFiles:` function.

What you should also see when you compare the two versions is that in the procedural version we have to check the kind of object we manipulate. In the object-oriented version, we simply tell the object to perform its own computation and return the result to us.

> **Important**   Don't ask, tell. Object-oriented programming essence is about sending order not checking state.

9.11   So far so good? Not fully!

We have a system with two classes and it offers some behavior composed out of well defined local behavior (see Figure 9-8). We can have objects composed out of other objects and messages flow within the graph. Object-oriented programming could stop here. Now it is annoying to have to duplicate structure and some methods between files and directories and this is what we will see when we will look at inheritance in Chapter 14. Inheritance is a mechanism to specialize incrementally classes from other classes.

9.12   Conclusion

- A class describes the state (instance variables) and the behavior (methods) of all its instances. The state of an instance is the value of its instance variables and it is specific to one single object while the behavior is shared by all the instances of a class.

- Different objects, instances of different classes, can react differently to the same messages.

- When sending a message, the associated method is found and executed.

CHAPTER 10

Converter

In this chapter you will implement a little temperature converter between celsius and fahrenheit degrees. It is so simple that it will help us to get started with Pharo and also with test driven development. Near the end of the chapter we will add logging facilities to the converter so that we can log the temperatures of certain locations. For this you will create a simple class and its tests.

We will show how to write test to specify the expected results. Writing tests is really important. It is one important tenet of Agile Programming and Test Driven Development (TDD). We will explain later why this is really good to have tests. For now we just implement them. We will also discuss a bit a fundamental aspects of float comparison and we will also present some loops.

10.1 First a test

First we define a test class named TemperatureConverterTest within the package MyConverter. It inherits from the class TestCase. This class is special, any method starting with 'test' will be executed automatically, one by one each time on a new instance of the class (to make sure that tests do not interfere with each others).

```
TestCase subclass: #TemperatureConverterTest
  instanceVariableNames: ''
  classVariableNames: ''
  package: 'MyConverter'
```

Converting from Fahrenheit to Celsius is done with a simple linear transformation. The formula to get Fahrenheit from Celsius is F = C * 1.8 + 32. Let us write a test covering such transformation. 30 Celsius should be 86 Fahrenheit.

```
testCelsiusToFahrenheit

    | converter |
    converter := TemperatureConverter new.
    self assert: ((converter convertCelsius: 30) = 86.0)
```

The test is structured the following way:

- Its selector starts with test, here the method is named testCelsiusToFahrenheit.

- It creates a new instance of TemperatureConverter (it is called the *context* of the test or more technically its fixture).

- Then we check using the message assert: that the expected behavior is really happening.

The message assert: expects a boolean. Here the expression ((converter convertCelsius: 30) = 86.0) returns a boolean. true if the converter returns the value 86.0, false otherwise.

The testing framework also offers some other similar methods. One is particularly interesting: assert:equals: makes the error reporting more user friendly. The previous method is strictly equivalent to the following one using assert:equals:.

```
testCelsiusToFahrenheit

    | converter |
    converter := TemperatureConverter new.
    self assert: (converter convertCelsius: 30) equals: 86.0
```

The message assert:equals: expects an expression and a result. Here (converter convertCelsius: 30) and 86.0. You can use the message you prefer and we suggest to use assert:equals: since it will help you to understand your mistake by saying: 'You expect 86.0 and I got 30' instead of simply telling you that the result is false.

10.2 Define a test method (and more)

While defining the method testCelsiusToFahrenheit using the class browser, the system will tell you that the class TemperatureConverter does not exist (This is true because we did not define it so far). The system will propose to create it. Just let the system do it.

Once you are done. You should have two classes: TemperatureConverterTest and TemperatureConverter. As well as one method: testCelsiusToFahrenheit. The test does not pass since we did not implement the

conversion method (as shown by the red color in the body of testCelsiusTo-
Fahrenheit).

Note that you entered the method above and the system compiled it. Now in
this book we want to make sure that you know about which method we are
talking about hence we will prefix the method definitions with their class.
For example the method testCelsiusToFahrenheit in the class TemperaturConverterTest is defined as follows:

```
TemperaturConverterTest >> testCelsiusToFahrenheit

  | converter |
  converter := TemperatureConverter new.
  self assert: (converter convertCelsius: 30) equals: 86.0
```

10.3   The class TemperaturConverter

The class TemperaturConverter is defined as shown below. You could have
define it before defining the class TemperaturConverterTest using the class
definition below:

```
Object subclass: #TemperatureConverter
  instanceVariableNames: ''
  classVariableNames: ''
  package: 'MyConverter'
```

This definition in essence, says that:

  • We want to define a new class named TemperaturConverter.

  • It has no instance or class variables (' ' means empty string).

  • It is packaged in package MyConverter.

Usually when doing Test Driven Development with Pharo, we focus on tests
and lets the system propose us some definitions. Then we can define the
method as follows.

```
TemperatureConverter >> convertCelsius: anInteger
  "Convert anInteger from celsius to fahrenheit"

  ^ ((anInteger * 1.8) + 32)
```

The system may tell you that the method is an utility method since it does
not use object state. It is a bit true because the converter is a *really* simple
object. For now do not care.

Your test should pass. Click on the icon close to the test method to execute
it.

10.4 **Converting from Farhenheit to Celsius**

Now you got the idea. Let us define a test for the conversion from Fahrenheit to Celsius.

```
TemperatureConverterTest >> testFahrenheitToCelsius

   | converter |
   converter := TemperatureConverter new.
   self assert: (converter convertFarhenheit: 86) equals: 30.0.
   self assert: (converter convertFarhenheit: 50) equals: 10
```

Define the method convertFarhenheit: anInteger

```
TemperatureConverter >> convertFarhenheit: anInteger
   "Convert anInteger from fahrenheit to celsius"

   ... Your solution ...
```

Run the tests they should all pass.

10.5 **About floats**

The conversions method we wrote returns floats. Floats are special objects in computer science because it is complex to represent infinite information (such as all the numbers between two consecutive integers) with a finite space (numbers are often represented with a fixed number of bits). In particular we should pay attention when comparing two floats. Here is a surprising case: we add two floats and the sum is not equal to their sums.

```
(0.1 + 0.2) = 0.3
> false
```

This is because the sum is not just equal to 0.3. The sum is in fact the number 0.30000000000000004

```
(0.1 + 0.2)
> 0.30000000000000004
```

To solve this problem in Pharo (it is the same in most programming languages), we do not use equality to compare floats but alternate messages such as closeTo: or closeTo:precision: as shown below:

```
(0.1 + 0.2) closeTo: 0.3
> true
(0.1 + 0.2) closeTo: 0.3 precision: 0.001
> true
```

To know more, you can have a look at the Fun with Float chapter in Deep Into Pharo (http://books.pharo.org)). The key point is that in computer science you should always avoid to compare the floats naively.

So let us go back to our conversion:

```
((52 - 32) / 1.8)
> 11.11111111111111
```

In the following expression we check that the result is close to 11.1 with a precision of 0.1. It means that we accept as result 11 or 11.1

```
((52 -  32) / 1.8) closeTo: 11.1 precision: 0.1
> true
```

We can use closeTo:precision: in our tests to make sure that we deal correctly with the float behavior we just described.

```
((52 -  32) / 1.8) closeTo: 11.1 precision: 0.1
> true
```

We change our tests to reflect this

```
TemperatureConverterTest >> testFahrenheitToCelsius

    | converter |
    converter := TemperatureConverter new.
    self assert: ((converter convertFarhenheit: 86) closeTo: 30.0
        precision: 0.1).
    self assert: ((converter convertFarhenheit: 50) closeTo: 10
        precision: 0.1)
```

10.6 Printing rounded results

The following expression shows that we may get converted temperature with a too verbose precision.

```
(TemperatureConverter new convertFarhenheit: 52)
>11.11111111111111
```

Here just getting 11.1 is enough. There is no need to get the full version. In fact, we can manipulate floats in full precision but there are case like User Interfaces where we would like to get a shorter sort of information. Typically as user of the temperature converter, our body does not see the difference between 12.1 or 12.2 degrees. Pharo libraries include the message printShowingDecimalPlaces: aNumberOfDigit used to round the *textual* representation of a float.

```
(TemperatureConverter new convertFarhenheit: 52)
    printShowingDecimalPlaces: 1
>11.1
```

10.7 Building a map of degrees

Often when you are travelling you would like to have kind of a map of different degrees as follows: Here we want to get the converted values between 50 to 70 fahrenheit degrees.

```
(TemperatureConverter new convertFarhenheitFrom: 50 to: 70 by: 2).
> { 50->10.0.
  52->11.1.
  54->12.2.
  56->13.3.
  58->14.4.
  60->15.6.
  62->16.7.
  64->17.8.
  66->18.9.
  68->20.0.
  70->21.1}
```

What we see is that the method convertFarhenheitFrom:to:by: returns an array of pairs.

A pair is created using the message -> and we can access the pair elements using the message key and value as shown below.

```
| p1 |
p1 := 50 -> 10.0.
p1 key
>>> 50
p1 value
>>> 10.0
```

Let us write a test first. We want to generate map containing as key the fahrenheit and as value the converted celsius. Therefore we will get a collection with the map named results and a collection of the expected values that the value of the elements should have.

On the two last lines of the test method, using the message with:do: we iterate on both collections in parallel taking on element of each collection and compare them.

```
TemperatureConverterTest >> testFToCScale

  | converter results expectedCelsius |
  converter := TemperatureConverter new.
  results := (converter convertFarhenheitFrom: 50 to: 70 by: 2).
  expectedCelsius := #(10.0 11.1 12.2 13.3 14.4 15.5 16.6 17.7 18.8
    20.0 21.1).

  results with: expectedCelsius
    do: [ :res :cel | res value closeTo: cel ]
```

Now we are ready to implement the method convertFarhenheitFrom: low to: high by: step. Using the message to:by:, we create an interval to generate the collection of numbers starting at low and ending up at high using the increment step. Then we use the message collect: which applies a block to a collection and returns a collection containing all the values returned by the block application. Here we just create a pair whose key is the fahrenheit and whose value is its converted celsius value.

```
TemperatureConverter >> convertFarhenheitFrom: low to: high by: step
   "Returns a collection of pairs (f, c) for all the fahrenheit
      temperatures from a low to an high temperature"

   ^ (low to: high by: step)
      collect: [ :f | f -> (self convertFarhenheit: f) ]
```

10.8 Spelling Fahrenheit correctly!

You may not noticed but we badly spelled fahrenheit since the beginning of this chapter! Fahrenheit is not spelt farhenheit but Fahrenheit. Now you may start to think that I'm crazy, because you should rename all the methods you wrote and in addition all the users of such methods and after we should check that we did not break anything. And you can think that this is a huge task.

Well first you should rename the methods because nobody wants to keep badly named code. Second, I'm not crazy at all. Programmers rename their code regularly because they often do not get it right the first time, or even the second time... Often you rewrite your code after thinking more about the interface you finally understand that you should propose. In fact good designer think a lot about names because names convey the intent of a computation. Now we have two super powerful tools to help us: Refactorings and Tests.

We will use the **Rename method** refactoring proposed by Pharo. A refactoring is a code transformation that preserves code properties. The Rename method refactoring garantees that not only the method but all the places where it is called will also be renamed to send the new message. In addition a refactoring garantees that the behavior of the program is not modified. So this is really powerful.

Select the method convertFarhenheit: in the method list and bring the menu, use the **Rename method (all)** item, give a new name convertFahrenheit:. The system will prompt you to show you all the corresponding operations. Check them to see what you should have done manually. Imagine the amount of mistakes you could have made and proceed. Do the same for convertFahrenheitFrom:to:by:.

Now the key question is if these changes broke anything. Normally everything should work since this is what we expect when using refactorings. But runnning the tests has the final word. So run the tests to check if everything is ok and here is a clear use of tests: they ensure that we can spot fast a regression.

With this little scenario you should have learned two important things:

- Tests are written once and executed million times to check for regression.

- Refactorings are really powerful operations that save us from tedious manual rewriting.

10.9 Adding logging behavior

Imagine now that you want to monitor the different temperatures between the locations where you live and where you work. (This is a real scenario since the building where my office is located got its heating broken over winter and I wanted to measure and keep a trace of the different temperatures in both locations.)

Here is a test representing a typical case. First, since I want to distinguish my measurements based on the locations, I added the possibility to specify a location. Then I want to be able to record temperatures either in celsius or in fahrenheit. Since the temperature often depends on the moment during the day I want to log the date and time with each measure.

Then we can request a converter for all the dates (message `dates`) and temperatures (message `temperatures`) that it contains.

```
TemperatureConverterTest >> testLocationAndDate

  | office |
  office := TemperatureConverter new location: 'Office'.
  "perform two measures that are logged"
  office measureCelsius: 19.
  office measureCelsius: 21.

  "We got effectively two measures"
  self assert: office measureCount = 2.

  "All the measures were done today"
  self assert: office dates equals: {Date today . Date today}
    asOrderedCollection.

  "We logged the correct temperature"
  self assert: office temperatures equals: { 19 . 21 }
    asOrderedCollection
```

The first thing that we do is to add two instance variables to our class: lo-cation that will hold the name of the location we measure and measures a collection that will hold all the temperatures and dates.

```
Object subclass: #TemperatureConverter
  instanceVariableNames: 'location measures'
  classVariableNames: ''
  package: 'MyConverter'
```

We initialize such variable with the following values.

```
TemperatureConverter >> initialize
  location := 'Nice'.
  measures := OrderedCollection new
```

It means that each instance will be able to have its own location and its own collection of measures. Now we are ready to record a temperature in celsius. What we do is that we add pair with the time and the value to our collection of measures.

```
TemperatureConverter >> measureCelsius: aTemp
  measures add: DateAndTime now -> aTemp
```

To support tests we also define a method returning the number of current measure our instance holds.

```
TemperatureConverter >> measureCount
  ... Your code ...
```

We now define three methods returning the sequence of temperatures, the dates and the times. Since the time has a microsecond precision it is a bit difficult to test. So we only test the dates.

```
TemperatureConverter >> temperatures
  ^ measures collect: [ :each | each value ]
```

To produce time without micro second we suggest to print the time using print24.

```
DateAndTime now asTime print24
>>> '22:46:33'
```

```
TemperatureConverter >> times
  ^ measures collect: [ :each | each key asTime ]
```

```
TemperatureConverter >> dates
  ... Your code ...
```

Now we can get two converters each with its own location and measurement records. The following tests verify that this is the case.

```
TemperatureConverterTest >> testTwoLocations

  | office home |
  office := TemperatureConverter new location: 'office'.
  office measureFahrenheit: 19.
  office measureFahrenheit: 21.
  self assert: office location equals: 'office'.
  self assert: office measureCount equals: 2.
  home := TemperatureConverter new location: 'home'.
  home measureFahrenheit: 22.
  home measureFahrenheit: 22.
  home measureFahrenheit: 22.
  self assert: home location equals: 'home'.
  self assert: home measureCount equals: 3.
```

We can add now a new method to convert fahrenheit to celcius and we define a new test first.

```
TemperatureConverterTest >> testLocationAndDateWithConversion

  | converter |
  converter := TemperatureConverter new location: 'Lille'.
  converter measureFahrenheit: 86.
  converter measureFahrenheit: 50.
  self assert: converter measureCount equals: 2.
  self assert: converter dates
    equals: {Date today . Date today} asOrderedCollection.
  self assert: converter temperatures
    equals: { converter convertFahrenheit: 86 .
        converter convertFahrenheit: 50 } asOrderedCollection
```

What we do is that since celsius is the scientific unity for temperature we convert to celsius before recording our temperature.

```
TemperatureConverter >> measureFahrenheit: aTemp
  ... Your code ...
```

10.10 Discussion

From a design perspective we see that the logger behavior is a much better object than the converter. The logger keeps some internal data specific to a location while the converter is stateless. Object-oriented programming is much better for capturing object with state. This is why the converter was a kind of silly objects but it was to get you started. Now it is rare that the world we want to model and represent is stateless. This is why object-oriented programming is a powerful way to develop complex programs.

10.11 **Conclusion**

In this chapter we built a simple temperature converter. We showed how define and execute unit tests using a Test Driven approach. The interest in testing and Test Driven Development is not limited to Pharo. Automated testing has become a hallmark of the *Agile software development* movement, and any software developer concerned with improving software quality would do well to adopt it.

We showed that tests are an important aid to measure our progress and also are an important aid to define clearly what we want to develop.

11

An electronic wallet

In this chapter you will develop a wallet. You will start by designing tests to define the behavior of our program, then we will define the methods according. Pay attention we will not give you all the solutions and the code.

11.1 A first test

Since we want to know if the code we will develop effectively does what it should do, we will write tests. A test can be as simple as verifying if our wallet contains money. To test that a newly created wallet does not contain money we can write a test as follow:

```
| w |
w := Wallet new.
w money = 0.
```

However doing it is tedious because we would have to manually run all the tests . We will use SUnit a system that automatically runs tests once we define them.

Our process will be the following one:

- imagine what we want to define
- define a test method
- execute it and check that it is failing
- define the method and fix it until the test pass.

With SUnit, tests are defined as methods inside a class subclass from Test-Case. So let us start to define a test class named WalletTest inside the package Wallet.

```
TestCase subclass: #WalletTest
  instanceVariableNames: ''
  classVariableNames: ''
  package: 'Wallet'
```

And now we can define a test. To define a test, we define a method starting with test. Here is the definition of the same test as before but using SUnit.

```
WalletTest >> testWalletAtCreationIsZero
  | w |
  w := Wallet new.
  self assert: w money = 0
```

Now executing a test can be done in different ways:

- click on the icon close to the method in class browser,

- use the TestRunner tools,

- execute WalletTest debug: #testWalletAtCreationIsZero or WalletTest run: #testWalletAtCreationIsZero

Now you should get started. Define the class Wallet inside the package Wallet.

```
Object subclass: #Wallet
  instanceVariableNames: ''
  classVariableNames: ''
  package: 'Wallet'
```

Run the test! It should be red and now define the method money. For now this method is plain stupid and will return 0. In the following of course it will sum all the coins and return such sum.

```
Wallet >> money
  ^ 0
```

11.2 Adding coins

Now we should be able to add coins to a wallet. Let us first define a new test testCoins.

```
WalletTest >> testCoins
  | w |
  w := Wallet new.
  w add: 2 coinsOfValue: 0.50.
  w add: 3 coinsOfValue: 0.20.
  self assert: w coinNumber = 5
```

The test adds several coins of different values and verifies that we did not lose any coins.

Now we should think how we will represent our wallet. We need to count how many coins of a given values are added or removed to a wallet. If we use an array or an ordered collection, we will have to maintain a mapping between the index and its corresponding value. Using a set will not really work since we will lose the occurrence of each coins.

11.3 Looking at Bag

A good structure to represent a wallet is a bag, instance of the class Bag: a bag keeps elements and their respective occurrences. Let us have a look at a bag example before continuing. You can add and remove elements of a bag and iterate on them. Let us play with it.

First we create a bag and we expect it to be empty:

```
| aFruitBag |
aFruitBag := Bag new.
aFruitBag size.
>>> 0
```

Then we add 3 bananas and verify that our bag really contains the three bananas we just added:

```
aFruitBag add: #Banana withOccurrences: 3.
aFruitBag size.
>>> 3
```

Now let us add different fruits:

```
aFruitBag add: #Apple withOccurrences: 10.
aFruitBag size.
>>> 13
```

Now we check that they are not mixed together.

```
aFruitBag occurrencesOf: #Apple.
>>> 10
```

We can also add a single fruit to our bag.

```
aFruitBag add: #Banana.
aFruitBag occurrencesOf: #Banana.
>>> 4
```

We can then iterate over all the contents of the bag using the message do:. The code snippet will print on the Transcript (open>Tools>Transcript) all the elements one by one.

```
7 timesRepeat: [aFruitBag remove: #Apple].
aFruitBag do: [ :each |  each logCr ].
```

```
#Banana
#Banana
#Banana
#Banana
#Apple
#Apple
#Apple
```

Since for an element we know its occurrence we can iterate differently as follows:

```
aFruitBag doWithOccurrences: [ :each :occurrence | ('There is ' ,
    occurrence printString , ' ', each ) logCr ]
```

We get the following trace in the Transcript.

```
'There is 4 Banana'
'There is 10 Apple'
```

We could change a bit the code to print correctly 'There is' and 'There are' depending on the occurrence. We left this as an exercise for you.

11.4 Using a bag for a wallet

Since we can know how many coins of a given value are in a bag, a bag is definitively a good structure for our wallet.

We will define add an instance variable bagCoins to the class and the methods

- add: anInteger coinsOfValue: aCoinNumber,
- initialize, and
- coinsOfValue:.

Let us start with the method initialize. We define the method initialize as follows. It is invoked automatically when an instance is created.

```
Wallet >> initialize
  bagCoins := Bag new
```

Now define the method add: anInteger coinsOfValue: aNumber. Browse the class Bag to find the messages that you can send to a bag.

```
Wallet >> add: anInteger coinsOfValue: aNumber
  "Add to the receiver, anInteger times a coin of value aNumber"

  ... Your solution ...
```

We can define the method coinsOfValue: that returns the number of coins of a given value (looks like the same as asking how many bananas are in the fruit bag).

```
Wallet >> coinsOfValue: aNumber

   ^ ... Your solution ...
```

11.5   More tests

The previous test is limited in the sense that we cannot distinguish if the coins are not mixed. It would be bad that a wallet would convert cents into euros. So let us define a new test to verify that the added coins are not mixed.

```
WalletTest >> testCoinsAddition
   | w |
   w := Wallet new.
   w add: 2 coinsOfValue: 0.50.
   w add: 3 coinsOfValue: 0.20.
   self assert: (w coinsOfValue: 0.5) = 2
```

We should also test that when we add twice the same coins they are effectively added.

```
WalletTest >> testCoinsAdditionISWorking
   | w |
   w := Wallet new.
   w add: 2 coinsOfValue: 0.50.
   w add: 6 coinsOfValue: 0.50.
   self assert: (w coinsOfValue: 0.5) = 8
```

11.6   Testing money

Now we can test that the money message returns the amount of money contained in the wallet and we should change the implementation of the money. We define two tests.

```
WalletTest >> testMoney
   | w |
   w := Wallet new.
   w add: 2 coinsOfValue: 0.50.
   w add: 3 coinsOfValue: 0.20.
   w add: 1 coinsOfValue: 0.02.
   self assert: w money = 1.62
```

```
WalletTest >> testMoney2
   | w |
   w := Wallet new.
   w add: 2 coinsOfValue: 0.50.
   w add: 3 coinsOfValue: 0.20.
   w add: 1 coinsOfValue: 0.02.
   w add: 5 coinsOfValue: 0.05.
   self assert: w money = 1.87
```

Now we should implement the method money.

```
Wallet >> money

   ^ ... Your solution ...
```

11.7 Checking to pay an amount

Now we can add a new message to know whether we can pay a certain amount.
But let us write some tests first.

```
WalletTest >> testCanPay
   | w |
   w := Wallet new.
   w add: 2 coinsOfValue: 0.50.
   w add: 3 coinsOfValue: 0.20.
   w add: 1 coinsOfValue: 0.02.
   w add: 5 coinsOfValue: 0.05.
   self assert: (w canPay: 2) not.
   self assert: (w canPay: 0.50).
```

Define the message canPay:.

```
Wallet >> canPay: amounOfMoney
   "returns true when we can pay the amount of money"

   ^ ... Your solution ...
```

11.8 Biggest coin

Now let us define a method to determine the largest coin in a wallet. We
write a test.

```
WalletTest >> testBiggestCoins
   | w |
   w := Wallet new.
   w add: 10 coinsOfValue: 0.50.
   w add: 10 coinsOfValue: 0.20.
   w add: 10 coinsOfValue: 0.10.
   self assert: w biggest equals: 0.50.
```

Note that the assert: message can also be replaced assert:equals: and
this is what we did: we replaced the expression self assert: w biggest =
0.5 by self assert: w biggest equals: 0.50.

Now we should define the method biggest.

```
Wallet >> biggest
  "Returns the biggest coin with a value below anAmount. For
     example, {(3 -> 0.5) . (3 -> 0.2) . (5-> 0.1)} biggest -> 0.5"

  ^ ... Your solution ...
```

11.9   Biggest below a value

We can also define the method `biggestBelow:` that returns the first coin whose value is strictly smaller than the argument. `{(3 -> 0.5) . (3 -> 0.2) . (5-> 0.1)} biggestBelow: 0.40` returns 0.2.

```
WalletTest >> testBiggestCoinsBelow
  | w |
  w := Wallet new.
  w add: 10 coinsOfValue: 0.50.
  w add: 10 coinsOfValue: 0.20.
  w add: 10 coinsOfValue: 0.10.
  self assert: (w biggestBelow: 1) equals: 0.50.
  self assert: (w biggestBelow: 0.5) equals: 0.20.
  self assert: (w biggestBelow: 0.48) equals: 0.20.
  self assert: (w biggestBelow: 0.20) equals: 0.10.
  self assert: (w biggestBelow: 0.10) equals: 0.
```

```
Wallet >> biggestBelow: anAmount
  "Returns the biggest coin with a value below anAmount. For
     example, {(3 -> 0.5) . (3 -> 0.2) . (5-> 0.1)} biggestBelow:
     0.40 -> 0.2"

  ^ ... Your solution ...
```

11.10   Improving the API

Better string representation

Now it is time to improve the API for our objects. First we should improve the way the wallet objects are printed so that we can debug more easily. For that we add the method `printOn:` aStream as follows:

```
Wallet >> printOn: aStream
  super printOn: aStream.
  aStream nextPutAll: ' (', self money asString, ')'
```

Easier addition

We can improve the API to add coins in particular when we add only one coin. So now you start to get used to it. We define a test.

```
WalletTest >> testAddOneCoin
  | w |
  w := Wallet new.
  w addCoin: 0.50.
  self assert: (w coinsOfValue: 0.5) = 1.
  self assert: w money equals: 0.5
```

Define the method addCoin:.

```
Wallet >> addCoin: aNumber
  "Add to the receiver a coin of value aNumber"

  ... Your solution ...
```

Removing coins

We can now implement the removal of a coin.

```
WalletTest >> testRemove
  | w |
  w := Wallet new.
  w add: 2 coinsOfValue: 0.50.
  w add: 3 coinsOfValue: 0.20.
  w add: 1 coinsOfValue: 0.02.
  w add: 5 coinsOfValue: 0.05.
  w removeCoin: 0.5.
  self assert: w money = 1.37
```

Define the method removeCoin:.

```
Wallet >> removeCoin: aCoinNumber
  "Remove from the receiver a coin of value aNumber"

  ... Your solution ...
```

We can generalize this behavior with a method remove:coinsOfValue:.
Write a test.

```
WalletTest >> testRemoveCoins
  | w |
  w := Wallet new.

  ... Your solution ...
```

```
Wallet >> remove: anInteger coinsOfValue: aCoin
  "Remove from the receiver, anInteger times a coin of value aNumber"

  bagCoins add: aCoin withOccurrences: anInteger
```

We can also define the method biggestAndRemove which removes the biggest
coin and returns it.

```
Wallet >> biggestAndRemove
  | b |
  b := self biggest.
  self removeCoin: b.
  ^ b
```

11.11   Coins for paying: First version

Now we would like to know the coins that we can use to pay a certain amount. We can define a method `coinsFor:` that will return a new wallet containing the coins to pay a given amount.

This is a more challenging task and we will propose a first version then we will add more complex situations and propose a more complex solution. So let us define a test.

```
WalletTest >> testCoinsForPaying

  | w paid |
  w := Wallet new.
  w add: 10 coinsOfValue: 0.50.
  w add: 10 coinsOfValue: 0.20.
  w add: 10 coinsOfValue: 0.10.
  paid := (w coinsFor: 2.5).
  self assert: paid money equals: 2.5.
  self assert: (paid coinsOfValue: 0.5) equals: 5
```

```
Wallet >> coinsFor: aValue
  "Returns a wallet with the largest coins to pay a certain amount
    and an empty wallet if this is not possible"

  | res |
  res := self class new.
  ^ (self canPay: aValue)
    ifFalse: [ res ]
    ifTrue: [ self coinsFor: aValue into: res ]
```

The method `coinsFor:` creates wallet and fill with the largest coins comprising a given value.

Using the previously defined methods, define a first version of the method `coinsFor: aValue into: accuWallet`.

```
Wallet >> coinsFor: aValue into: accuWallet

  ... Your solution ...
```

Here is a possible simple solution: we remove from the wallet the largest coin and we add it to the resulting wallet. This solution is not working well as we will show it.

```
Wallet >> coinsFor: aValue into: accuWallet

  [ accuWallet money < self money ]
      whileTrue: [ accuWallet addCoin: self biggestAndRemove ].
  ^ accuWallet
```

11.12 Better heuristics

Let us try some tests to see if our previous way to get coins is working. (The previous algorithm does not work with such behavior.)

The first test checks that when there is no more coins of the biggest value, we check that the next coin is then used.

```
WalletTest >> testCoinsForPayingWithOtherCoins
  | w paid |
  w := Wallet new.
  w add: 1 coinsOfValue: 0.50.
  w add: 10 coinsOfValue: 0.20.
  w add: 10 coinsOfValue: 0.10.
  paid := (w coinsFor: 2.4).
  self assert: paid money equals: 2.4.
  self assert: (paid coinsOfValue: 0.5) equals: 1.
  self assert: (paid coinsOfValue: 0.2) equals: 9.
```

Run the tests and define the method coinsFor: to invoke a copy of the method coinsFor: aValue into: accuWallet renamed coinsFor: aValue into2: accuWallet to start with.

```
Wallet >> coinsFor: aValue
  "Returns a wallet with the largest coins to pay a certain amount
    and an empty wallet if this is not possible"
  | res |
  res := self class new.
  ^ (self canPay: aValue)
    ifFalse: [ res ]
    ifTrue: [ self coinsFor: aValue into2: res ]
```

The previous algorithm (implemented above in coinsFor: aValue into:) does not work with such behavior. So you should start to address the problem and add more and more tests. The second test checks that even if there is a coin with a largest value, the algorithm selects the next one. Here to pay 0.6, we should get 0.5 then we should not take 0.2 the next coin but 0.1 instead.

```
WalletTest >> testCoinsForPayingWithOtherThanTop
  | w paid |
  w := Wallet new.
  w add: 1 coinsOfValue: 0.50.
  w add: 10 coinsOfValue: 0.20.
```

```
w add: 10 coinsOfValue: 0.10.
paid := (w coinsFor: 0.6).
self assert: paid money equals: 0.6.
self assert: (paid coinsOfValue: 0.5) equals: 1.
self assert: (paid coinsOfValue: 0.1) equals: 1.
```

In this version we check that the algorithm should skip multiple coins that are available. In the example, for 0.6 it should select: 0.5 then skip the remaining 0.5, and 0.2 to get one 0.1.

```
WalletTest >> testCoinsForPayingWithOtherThanTopMoreDifficult
  | w paid |
  w := Wallet new.
  w add: 2 coinsOfValue: 0.50.
  w add: 10 coinsOfValue: 0.20.
  w add: 10 coinsOfValue: 0.10.
  paid := (w coinsFor: 0.6).
  self assert: paid money equals: 0.6.
  self assert: (paid coinsOfValue: 0.5) equals: 1.
  self assert: (paid coinsOfValue: 0.1) equals: 1.
```

The following one is a variant of the previous test where the biggest coin should be skipped.

```
WalletTest >> testCoinsForPayingWithOtherThanTopMoreDifficult2
  | w paid |
  w := Wallet new.
  w add: 1 coinsOfValue: 1.
  w add: 2 coinsOfValue: 0.50.
  w add: 10 coinsOfValue: 0.20.
  w add: 10 coinsOfValue: 0.10.
  paid := (w coinsFor: 0.6).
  self assert: paid money equals: 0.6.
  self assert: (paid coinsOfValue: 0.5) equals: 1.
  self assert: (paid coinsOfValue: 0.1) equals: 1.
```

11.13 Conclusion

What this example shows is that while a wallet is essentially a bag, having a wallet is a much more powerful solution. The wallet encapsulates an internal representation and builds a more complex API around it.

CHAPTER 12

Crafting a simple embedded DSL with Pharo

In this chapter you will develop a simple domain specific language (DSL) for rolling dice. Players of games such as Dungeons & Dragons are familiar with such DSL. An example of such DSL is the following expression: 2 D20 + 1 D6 which means that we should roll two 20-faces dices and one 6 faces die. It is called an embedded DSL because the DSL uses the syntax of the language used to implement it. Here we use the Pharo syntax to implement the Dungeons & Dragons rolling die language.

This little exercise shows how we can (1) simply reuse traditional operator such as +, (2) develop an embedded domain specific language and (3) use class extensions (the fact that we can define a method in another package than the one of the class of the method).

12.1 Getting started

Using the code browser, define a package named Dice or any name you like.

Create a test

It is always empowering to verify that the code we write is always working as we defining it. For this purpose you should create a unit test. Remember unit testing was promoted by K. Beck first in the ancestor of Pharo. Nowadays this is a common practice but this is always useful to remember our roots!

Define the class DieTest as a subclass of TestCase as follows:

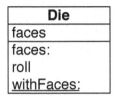

Figure 12-1 A single class with a couple of messages. Note that the method withFaces: is a class method.

```
TestCase subclass: #DieTest
    instanceVariableNames: ''
    classVariableNames: ''
    package: 'Dice'
```

What we can test is that the default number of faces of a die is 6.

```
DieTest >> testInitializeIsOk
    self assert: Die new faces equals: 6
```

If you execute the test, the system will prompt you to create a class Die. Do it.

Define the class Die

The class Die inherits from Object and it has an instance variable, faces to represent the number of faces one instance will have. Figure 12-1 gives an overview of the messages.

```
Object subclass:
    ... Your solution ...
```

In the initialization protocol, define the method initialize so that it simply sets the default number of faces to 6.

```
Die >> initialize
    ... Your solution ...
```

Do not hesitate to add a class comment.

Now define a method to return the number of faces an instance of Die has.

```
Die >> faces
    ^ faces
```

Now your tests should all pass (and turn green).

Figure 12-2   Inspecting and interacting with a die.

12.2   **Rolling a die**

To roll a die you should use the method from Number atRandom which draws randomly a number between one and the receiver. For example 10 atRandom draws number between 1 to 10. Therefore we define the method roll:

```
Die >> roll
    ... Your solution ...
```

Now we can create an instance Die new and send it the message roll and get a result. Do Die new inspect to get an inspector and then type in the bottom pane self roll. You should get an inspector like the one shown in Figure 12-2. With it you can interact with a die by writing expression in the bottom pane.

12.3   **Creating another test**

But better, let us define a test that verifies that rolling a new created dice with a default 6 faces only returns value comprised between 1 and 6. This is what the following test method is actually specifying.

```
DieTest >> testRolling
    | d |
    d := Die new.
    10 timesRepeat: [ self assert: (d roll between: 1 and: 6) ]
```

> **Important**   Often it is better to define the test even before the code it tests. Why? Because you can think about the API of your objects and a scenario that illustrate their correct behavior. It helps you to program your solution.

12.4 Instance creation interface

We would like to get a simpler way to create Die instances. For example we want to create a 20-faces die as follows: Die withFaces: 20 instead of always have to send the new message to the class as in Die new faces: 20. Both expressions are creating the same die but one is shorter.

Let us look at it:

- In the expression Die withFaces:, the message withFaces: is sent to the class Die. It is not new, we constantly sent the message new to Die to created instances.

- Therefore we should define a method that will be executed

Let us define a test for it.

```
DieTest >> testCreationIsOk
  self assert: (Die withFaces: 20) faces equals: 20
```

What the test clearly shows is that we are sending a message to the **class** Die itself.

Defining a class method

Define the *class* method withFaces: as follows:

- Click on the class button in the browser to make sure that you are editing a **class** method.

- Define the method as follows:

```
Die class >> withFaces: aNumber
  "Create and initialize a new die with aNumber faces."
  | instance |
  instance := self new.
  instance faces: aNumber.
  ^ instance
```

Let us explain this method

- The method withFaces: creates an instance using the message new. Since self represents the receiver of the message and the receiver of the message is the class Die itself then self represents the class Die.

- Then the method sends the message faces: to the instance and

- Finally returns the newly created instance.

Pay really attention that a class method withFaces: is sent to a class, and an instance method sent to the newly created instance faces:. Note that the class method could have also named faces: or any name we want, it does not matter, it is executed when the receiver is the class Die.

If you execute it will not work since we did not create yet the method `faces:`. This is now the time to define it. Pay attention the method `faces:` is sent to an instance of the class `Die` and not the class itself. It is an instance method, therefore make sure that you deselected the class button before editing it.

```
Die >> faces: aNumber
  faces := aNumber
```

Now your tests should run. So even if the class `Die` could implement more behavior, we are ready to implement a die handle.

> **Important**   A class method is a method executed in reaction to messages sent to a *class*. It is defined on the class side of the class. In `Die with-Faces: 20`, the message `withFaces:` is sent to the class `Die`. In `Die new faces: 20`, the message `new` is sent to the *class* `Die` and the message `faces:` is sent to the *instance* returned by `Die new`.

[Optional] Alternate instance creation definition

In a first reading you can skip this section. The *class* method definition `with-Faces:` above is strictly equivalent to the one below.

```
Die class >> withFaces: aNumber
  ^ self new faces: aNumber; yourself
```

Let us explain it a bit. `self` represents the class `Die` itself. Sending it the message `new`, we create an instance and send it the `faces:` message. And we return the expression. So why do we need the message `yourself`. The message `yourself` is needed to make sure that whatever value the instance message `faces:` returns, the instance creation method we are defining returns the new created instance. You can try to redefine the instance method `faces:` as follows:

```
Die >> faces: aNumber
  faces := aNumber.
  ^ 33
```

Without the use of `yourself`, `Die withFaces: 20` will return 33. With `yourself` it will return the instance.

The trick is that `yourself` is a simple method defined on `Object` class: The message `yourself` returns the receiver of a message. The use of `;` sends the message to the receiver of the previous message (here `faces:`). The message `yourself` is then sent to the object resulting from the execution of the expression `self new` (which returns a new instance of the class `Die`), as a consequence it returns the new instance.

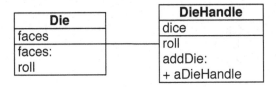

Figure 12-3 A die handle is composed of dice.

12.5 First specification of a die handle

Let us define a new class `DieHandle` that represents a die handle. Here is the API that we would like to offer for now (as shown in Figure 12-3). We create a new handle then add some dice to it.

```
DieHandle new
  addDie: (Die withFaces: 6);
  addDie: (Die withFaces: 10);
  yourself
```

Of course we will define tests first for this new class. We define the class `DieHandleTest`.

```
TestCase subclass: #DieHandleTest
  instanceVariableNames: ''
  classVariableNames: ''
  package: 'Dice'
```

Testing a die handle

We define a new test method as follows. We create a new handle and add one die of 6 faces and one die of 10 faces. We verify that the handle is composed of two dice.

```
DieHandleTest >> testCreationAdding
  | handle |
  handle := DieHandle new
      addDie: (Die withFaces: 6);
      addDie: (Die withFaces: 10);
      yourself.
  self assert: handle diceNumber = 2.
```

In fact we can do it better. Let us add a new test method to verify that we can even add two dice having the same number of faces.

```
DieHandleTest >> testAddingTwiceTheSameDice
  | handle |
  handle := DieHandle new.
  handle addDie: (Die withFaces: 6).
  self assert: handle diceNumber = 1.
```

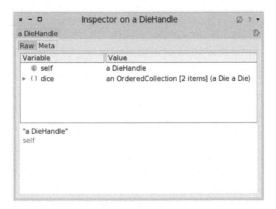

Figure 12-4   Inspecting a DieHandle.

```
handle addDie: (Die withFaces: 6).
self assert: handle diceNumber = 2.
```

Now that we specified what we want, we should implement the expected class and messages. Easy!

12.6   Defining the DieHandle class

The class DieHandle inherits from Object and it defines one instance variable to hold the dice it contains.

```
Object subclass: ...
   ... Your solution ...
```

We simply initialize it so that its instance variable dice contains an instance of OrderedCollection.

```
DieHandle >> initialize
   ... Your solution ...
```

Then define a simple method addDie: to add a die to the list of dice of the handle. You can use the message add: sent to a collection.

```
DieHandle >> addDie: aDie
   ... Your solution ...
```

Now you can execute the code snippet and inspect it. You should get an inspector as shown in Figure 12-4

```
DieHandle new
   addDie: (Die withFaces: 6);
   addDie: (Die withFaces: 10);
   yourself
```

Finally we should add the method `diceNumber` to the `DieHandle` class to be able to get the number of dice of the handle. We just return the size of the dice collection.

```
DieHandle >> diceNumber
    ^ dice size
```

Now your tests should run and this is a good moment to save and publish your code.

12.7 Improving programmer experience

Now when you open an inspector you cannot see well the dice that compose the die handle. Click on the `dice` instance variable and you will only get a list of a `Dice` without further information. What we would like to get is something like a `Die (6)` or a `Die (10)` so that in a glance we know the faces a die has.

```
DieHandle new
    addDie: (Die withFaces: 6);
    addDie: (Die withFaces: 10);
    yourself
```

This is the message `printOn:` that is responsible to provide a textual representation of the message receiver. By default, it just prints the name of the class prefixed with 'a' or 'an'. So we will enhance the `printOn:` method of the `Die` class to provide more information. Here we simply add the number of faces surrounded by parenthesis. The `printOn:` message is sent with a stream as argument. This is in such stream that we should add information. We use the message `nextPutAll:` to add a number of characters to the stream. We concatenate the characters to compose ( ) using the message , comma defined on collections (and that concatenate collections and strings).

```
Die >> printOn: aStream

    super printOn: aStream.
    aStream nextPutAll: ' (', faces printString, ')'
```

Now in your inspector you can see effectively the number of faces a die handle has as shown by Figure 12-5 and it is now easier to check the dice contained inside a handle (See Figure 12-6).

12.8 Rolling a die handle

Now we can define the rolling of a die handle by simply summing result of rolling each of its dice. Implement the `roll` method of the `DieHandle` class. This method must collect the results of rolling each dice of the handle and sum them.

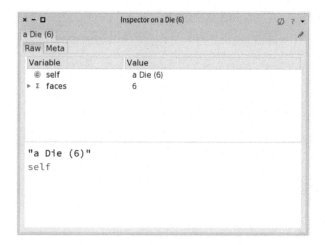

Figure 12-5 Die details.

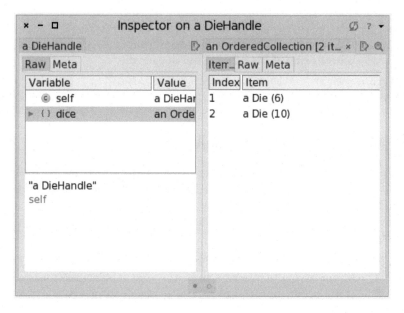

Figure 12-6 A die handle with more information.

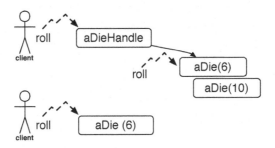

Figure 12-7 A polymorphic API supports the *Don't ask, tell* principle.

You may want to have a look at the method sum in the class Collection or use a simple loop.

```
DieHandle >> roll
    ... Your solution ...
```

Now we can send the message roll to a die handle.

```
handle := DieHandle new
    addDie: (Die withFaces: 6);
    addDie: (Die withFaces: 10);
    yourself.
handle roll
```

Define a test to cover such behavior. Rolling an handle of n dice should be between n and the sum of the face number of each die.

```
DieHandleTest >> testRoll
    ... Your solution ...
```

12.9 About Dice and DieHandle API

It is worth to spend some times looking at the relationship between DieHandle and Dice. A die handle is composed of dices. What is an important design decision is that the API of the main behavior (roll) is the same for a die or a die handle. You can send the message roll to a dice or a die handle. This is an important property.

Why? Because it means that from a client perspective, she/he can treat the receiver without having to take care about the kind of object it is manipulating. A client just sends the message roll to an object and get back a number (as shown in Figure 12-7). The client is not concerned by the fact that the receiver is composed out a simple object or a complex one. Such design decision supports the *Don't ask, tell* principle.

> **Important**   Offering polymorphic API is a tenet of good object-oriented design. It enforces the *Don't ask, tell* principle. Clients do not have to worry about the type of the objects to whom they talk to.

For example we can write the following expression that adds a die and a dieHandle to a collection and collect the different values (we convert the result into an array so that we can print it in the book).

```
| col |
col := OrderedCollection new.
col add: (Die withFaces: 20).
col add: (DieHandle new addDie: (Die withFaces: 4); yourself).
(col collect: [:each | each roll]) asArray
>>> #(17 3)
```

About composition

Composite objects such document objects (a book is composed of chapters, a chapter is composed of sections, a section is composed of paragraphs) have often a more complex composition relationship than the composition between die and die handle. Often the composition is recursive in the sense that an element can be the whole: for example, a diagram can be composed of lines, circles, and other diagrams. We will see an example of such composition in the Expression Chapter 16.

12.10   Role playing syntax

Now we are ready to offer a syntax following practice of role playing game, i.e., using 2 D20 to create a handle of two dice with 20 faces each. For this purpose we will define class extensions: we will define methods in the class Integer but these methods will be only available when the package Dice will be loaded.

But first let us specify what we would like to obtain by writing a new test in the class DieHandleTest. Remember to always take any opportunity to write tests. When we execute 2 D20 we should get a new handle composed of two dice and can verify that. This is what the method testSimpleHandle is doing.

```
DieHandleTest >> testSimpleHandle
  self assert: 2 D20 diceNumber = 2.
```

Verify that the test is not working! It is much more satisfactory to get a test running when it was not working before. Now define the method D20 with a protocol named *NameOfYourPackage ('*Dice' if you named your package 'Dice'). The * (star) prefixing a protocol name indicates that the protocol and its methods belong to another package than the package of the class.

Here we want to say that while the method D20 is defined in the class Integer, it should be saved with the package Dice.

The method D20 simply creates a new die handle, adds the correct number of dice to this handle, and returns the handle.

```
Integer >> D20
    ... Your solution ...
```

About class extensions

We asked you to place the method D20 in a protocol starting with a star and having the name of the package ('*Dice') because we want this method to be saved (and packaged) together with the code of the classes we already created (Die, DieHandle,...) Indeed in Pharo we can define methods in classes that are not defined in our package. Pharoers call this action a class extension: we can add methods to a class that is not ours. For example D20 is defined on the class Integer. Now such methods only make sense when the package Dice is loaded. This is why we want to save and load such methods with the package we created. This is why we are defining the protocol as '*Dice'. This notation is a way for the system to know that it should save the methods with the package and not with the package of the class Integer.

Now your tests should pass and this is probably a good moment to save your work either by publishing your package and to save your image.

We can do the same for the default dice with different faces number: 4, 6, 10, and 20. But we should avoid duplicating logic and code. So first we will introduce a new method D: and based on it we will define all the others.

Make sure that all the new methods are placed in the protocol '*Dice'. To verify you can press the button Browse of the Monticello package browser and you should see the methods defined in the class Integer.

```
Integer >> D: anInteger
    ... Your solution ...
Integer >> D4
    ^ self D: 4
Integer >> D6
    ^ self D: 6
Integer >> D10
    ^ self D: 10
Integer >> D20
    ^ self D: 20
```

We have now a compact form to create dice and we are ready for the last part: the addition of handles.

12.11 Handle's addition

Now what is missing is that possibility to add several handles as follows: 2 D20 + 3 D10. Of course let's write a test first to be clear on what we mean.

```
DieHandleTest >> testSumming
    | handle |
    handle := 2 D20 + 3 D10.
    self assert: handle diceNumber = 5.
```

We will define a method + on the HandleDice class. In other languages this is often not possible or is based on operator overloading. In Pharo + is just a message as any other, therefore we can define it on the classes we want.

Now we should ask ourself what is the semantics of adding two handles. Should we modify the receiver of the expression or create a new one. We preferred a more functional style and choose to create a third one.

The method + creates a new handle then add to it the dice of the receiver and the one of the handle passed as argument to the message. Finally we return it.

```
DieHandle >> + aDieHandle
    ... Your solution ...
```

Now we can execute the method (2 D20 + 1 D6) roll nicely and start playing role playing games, of course.

12.12 Conclusion

This chapter illustrates how to create a small DSL based on the definition of some domain classes (here Dice and DieHandle) and the extension of core class such as Integer. It also shows that we can create packages with all the methods that are needed even when such methods are defined on classes external (here Integer) to the package. It shows that in Pharo we can use usual operators such as + to express natural models.

Part III

Sending messages

13

Sending a message is making a choice

In this chapter we explore an *essential* point of object-oriented programming: Sending a message is making a choice!

Object-oriented programming books often present *late binding*: the fact that the method to execute will only be determined at runtime based on the receiver. In fact sending a message uses late binding to select the correct method. I like to use the term *sending a message* because it stresses that simple actions, such as sending a message, are also a powerful feature when used well.

This aspect is often not really well put in perspective in teaching materials. Lectures often focus on inheritance but understanding the power of message passing it crucial to build good design. This point is so central for me that this is the first point that I explain when I start lectures on advanced design to people already understanding object-oriented programming. In addition, most of the Design Patterns are based on the fact that sending a message is actually selecting the correct method based on the message receiver.

To illustrate how sending a message performs a dynamic choice, I will start taking a simple example available in the core of Pharo: the Booleans. Pharo defines Booleans as two objects: `true` and `false`. They are so fundamental that you cannot change their value. Still their implementation also use late binding in a really elegant way. I will explain how the Boolean negation and the disjunction (or) are implemented. Then I will step back and analyse the forces in presence and their importance.

13.1 Negation: the not message

Boolean negation has nothing special in Pharo: negating a boolean returned the negated value! For example the snippets below show this conventional behavior and vice versa.

Sending the message not to the Boolean true returns the Boolean false.

```
true not
>>> false
```

```
false not
>>> true
```

Nothing fancy. Of course the message not can be sent to Boolean expressions (i.e. expressions whose execution return Booleans) as shown below:

```
(2 * 4 > 3) not
>>> false
```

```
(#(1 2 3) includes: 5) not
>>> true
```

Now while Pharo follows traditional Boolean logic, what is less traditional is the implementation of the way the computation is done to answer the correct value.

13.2 Implementing not

Take a couple of minutes and a piece of paper and think about the way you would implement this message. Try really to write the code for real.

A first hint.

A first hint that I can give you is that the solution (used in Pharo and that we want to study) does not use explicit conditional such as ifTrue: or ifTrue:if-False:.

Take a bit more time to think how you can implement not. What we can tell you is the solution is not based on bit fiddling and logical operation on small integers. The solution we are looking for is simple and elegant.

A second hint.

The second hint is that true and false are instances of different classes. true is (the unique) instance of the class True while false is (the unique) instance of the class False. Note the uppercase on class names. This situation is depicted in Figure 13-1.

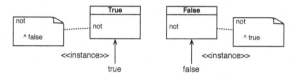

Figure 13-1   The two classes True and False and their respective unique instances true and false.

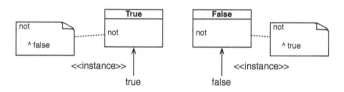

Figure 13-2   Two methods for one message.

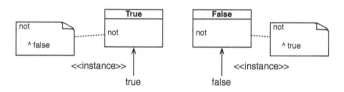

Figure 13-3   Two methods for one message each one returning the other instance.

What you should see is that the fact that the solution has two different classes opens the door to have two different not implementations as shown by Figure 13-2. Indeed, as we mention in early chapters, we can have one message and multiple methods that we will be selected and executed depending on the receiver of the message.

Now you should be ready to get the solution. We should have a definition for the true defined in the class True and one for false in the class False.

Studying the implementation

The implementation of negation (message not) is defined as illustrated in Figure 13-3 and is shown below. The method not of the class True simply returns the Boolean false.

```
True >> not
    "Negation--answer false since the receiver is true."
    ^ false
```

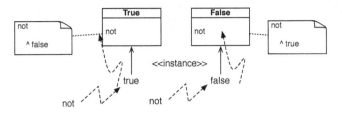

Figure 13-4 Sending a message selects the method in the class of the receiver.

```
False >> not
    "Negation--answer true since the receiver is false."
    ^ true
```

Figure 13-4 shows that sending a message to one of the two Booleans selects the method in the corresponding class. What is important to see is that when a method is executed the receiver is from the class (or subclass we will see that later) that defines the method. We can also say that when we define a method in a given class we know that the receiver is from this class. Obvious, isn't it! But important. The implementation can then use this information as an execution context. This is exactly what the not implementation does. The method not defined on the class True knows that the receiver is true so it just has to return false.

> **Note** When we define a method in a given class we know that the receiver is from this class. Obvious but important. The implementation can then use this information.

Now we will see if you get it... Let us try with a slightly more complex example.

13.3 Implementing disjunction

Disjunction is also a core functionality of any programming language. In Pharo disjunction is expressed via the message |. Here are the traditional tables describing disjunction but expressed in Pharo: first starting with true as receiver.

or	true	false
true	true	true
false	true	false

Here are a couple of examples expressed in Pharo.

```
true | true
>>> true
```

```
true | false
>>> true
```

```
false | false
>>> false
```

For the record, in fact the message | implements an eager disjunction since it asks the value of its argument even when not needed and Pharo also offers lazy disjunction implemented in the message or: which only requests the argument value if needed.

When receiver is true.

Propose an implementation of the disjunction for the first case: i.e. when the receiver is the object true.

or	true	false
true	true	true

What you should have learned from the implementation of not is that you have two different methods taking advantage of the fact that they know what is the receiver during their execution.

```
true | true
>>> true
```

```
true | false
>>> true
```

```
true | anything
>>> true
```

When you look at the table we see that when the receiver is true the result is the same as the receiver (i.e. true). In Pharo the method | on class True express this as follows:

```
True >> | aBoolean
    "Evaluating Or -- answer true since the receiver is true."
    ^ true
```

When receiver is false.

Similarly let us study the Boolean table relative to false as receiver.

or	true	false
false	true	false

Here are some snippets

```
false | true
>>> true
```

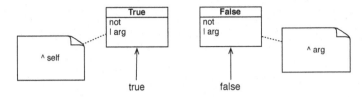

Figure 13-5 Disjunction implementation: two methods.

```
false | false
>>> false
```

```
false | anything
>>> anything
```

We see that when the receiver is false, the result of the disjunction is the other argument. In Pharo the method | on class False is then as follows:

```
False >> | aBoolean
    "Evaluating Or -- answer with the argument, aBoolean."
    ^ aBoolean
```

13.4 About ifTrue:ifFalse: implementation

Now you should start to get the principle. Let us see how it works to also express conditional messages such as ifTrue:ifFalse:. Yes fundamental messages such as conditionals can be expressed using the same mechanism: late binding.

What you see with the following snippet is that message ifTrue:ifFalse: is expecting two different blocks as argument.

```
4 factorial > 20
  ifTrue: [ 'bigger' ]
  ifFalse: [ 'smaller' ]
>>> 'bigger'
```

Now you should know that to execute a block you should use the message value as illustrated:

```
[1 + 3] value
>>> 4
```

Block can contain any expressions. The execution of the following block will open the Pharo logo.

```
[ (ZnEasy getPng: 'http://pharo.org/web/files/pharo.png')
        asMorph openInWindow ] value
```

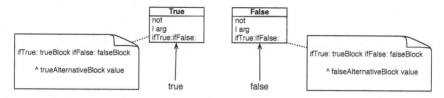

Figure 13-6 Conditional implementation: again two methods and no explicit tests.

Let us come back to the case of condition and in particular to the message ifTrue:ifFalse:. Based on the receiver we should execute the corresponding block from the ifTrue:ifFalse: method. When the expression (4 factorial > 20 in the example above) is true we should execute the ifTrue: argument, when it is false we should execute the ifFalse: argument.

Implementation.

The implementations is then simple and elegant. In the True class, we want to execute the corresponding block, the one passed as ifTrue: argument as shown in Figure 13-6.

```
True >> ifTrue: trueAlternativeBlock ifFalse: falseAlternativeBlock
    ^ trueAlternativeBlock value
```

Similarly in the False class, we want to execute the corresponding block, the one passed as ifFalse: argument.

```
False >> ifTrue: trueAlternativeBlock ifFalse: falseAlternativeBlock
    ^ falseAlternativeBlock value
```

Optimisation.

What we show above works! But if you modify it, the modification will not be taken into account. This is because in Pharo ifTrue:ifFalse: is used so often and its semantics should not change that the compiler in fact does not send a message but convert it in low-level logic for the virtual machine. Now you can invent your own conditional message siVrai:siFaux: for a french version for example and you will see that this implementation works.

13.5 What is the point?

Some readers may be intrigued and think that this is spurious because they will never have to reimplement Booleans in their life. This is true even if there are different versions of Boolean logic such as the ternary logic that contains also unknown value.

We picked the Boolean examples to illustrate an important point: sending a message is making a choice. The runtime system will dynamically select the method depending on the receiver. This is what is called late binding or dynamic dispatch. Only at execution the correct method is selected. Now the Boolean example is the simplest one I could find to illustrate this point. It is also ground breaking in the sense that it touches something as fundamental as Boolean main operations.

Now the choices can be made over several dozens of classes. For example in Pillar the document processing system in which this book is written there are around 59 different classes expressing different parts of a document: section, title, bold, paragraph... and the same principle applies there. The system selects the correct methods to render text, LaTeX or HTML using exactly the same principle.

Now most of the time you can express the same using conditions (except for the Boolean example and this is why I asked you to implement Boolean logic since you do not want to have Boolean logic to be based on condition because this is inefficient) as follows:

```
emitHTML: stream
  self == PRList
    ifTrue: [ ... ]
    self == PRParagraph
      ifTrue: [ ... ]
      ...
```

The problems with such explicit conditions is the following:

- First, they are cumbersome to write. Even using case statements as in other languages, the logic can become complex. Imagine for 59 cases of Pillar. Here is a small part of the document hierarchy.

```
PRObject #(''properties'')
        PRDocumentItem #(''counter'')
              PRDocumentGroup #(''children'')
                    PRDocument #()
                    PRHeader #(''level'')
                    PRList #()
                            PROrderedList #()
                            PRUnorderedList #()
                    PRParagraph #()
                    PRReference #(''reference'' ''parameters'')
                            PRFigure #()
                    PRSlide #(''title'' ''label'')
              PRText #(''text'')'
```

- Second, such definitions are not modular. It means that adding a new case requires to edit the method and recompile it. While with the dynamic dispatch, we can just add a new class as shown in Figure 13-7.

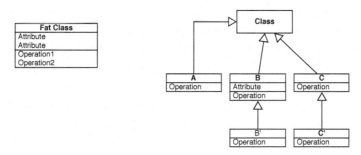

Figure 13-7   One single class vs. a nice hierarchy.

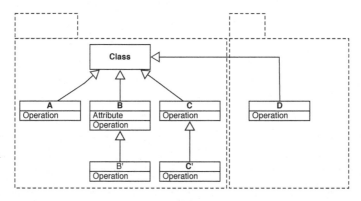

Figure 13-8   One single class vs. a nice hierarchy.

Furthermore this class can just take advantage of an existing one and
extend it (as we will explained in Chapter 14).

You could think that this is a not a problem but imagine that now for a busi-
ness you want to ship different products or solutions to your clients. With
dynamic dispatch you can simply package alternate code in separate packages and load them independently as shown in Figure 13-8.

Classes represent choices

Sending a message is making a choice. Now the following question is which
elements represent choices. Because you can have the possibility to chose
something but if there is only one choice you will not go that far and take
advantage of the power of late binding.

In fact classes represent choices. In the Boolean case you have two choices
one for true and one for false. There is a really difference for example between the FatClass design (left in Figure 13-7) and the modular design (right
in Figure 13-7) because we see all the choices which can be made at runtime

in the latter case.

When I do code review, I looked at how domain variations are represented and if there are enough classes. What is important to realise is that classes are cheap. It is better to write 5 little classes than a huge one. Some (even smart) people get confused by measuring complexity of a system using number of classes. Having many classes representing good abstractions with a single responsibility is much better than having a single class exhibiting multiple responsibilities.

13.6 Conclusion

Sending a message is really powerful since it selects the adequate method to be executed on the receiver. Now this is even more powerful than that: Remember that when we execute a method, one key information we have at hand is that the receiver is an instance from this class (or one of its subclasses as we will see later) and we can take advantage of this information to eliminate tests. Indeed an object executes a method that have been designed to be executed on it. So no need to test more.

Now you should start to understand why in Pharo we are picky about the vocabulary: we use sending a message and not calling a method as in other language. Because sending a message conveys much better the idea that the correct method will be selected and that we do not know a priori which one will be executed.

In future chapters we will show that sending a message is creating in fact a hook so that other methods can be executed in place.

Part IV

Looking at inheritance

CHAPTER **14** ■

Inheritance: Incremental definition and behavior reuse

In Chapter 8, we presented objects and classes. Objects are entities that communicate exclusively by sending and receiving messages. Objects are described by classes that are factories of objects. Classes define behavior and structure of all their instances: All the instances of a class share the same behavior but have their own private state.

In this chapter we present the fundamental concept of *inheritance* that allows a class to reuse and extend the behavior of another class. The idea is that as a programmer we do not want to rewrite from scratch a functionality if another class already offers it. A programm specialises the implemented behavior into the new behavior he wants. Inheritance lets us express this concept specialisation. Using inheritance we create trees of concepts where more precise ones refine more abstract and generic ones.

Inheritance is based on dynamic method lookup: a method is looked up dynamically within the inheritance tree starting from the class of the receiver. Once this explained we will show that it is possible to get code of a subclass invoked in place of the one of a superclass.

To illustrate the important points of inheritance, we revisit the example of Chapter 8.

14.1 Inheritance

Object-oriented programming is also based on the *incremental* definition of abstractions. This *incremental* definition mechanism is central to support reuse and extension of abstraction. It is called *inheritance*. The idea is that

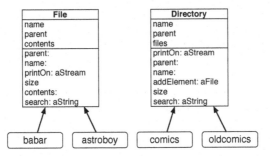

Figure 14-1 Two classes understanding similar sets of messages and structuring their instances in a similar way.

you can define a new abstraction (a class) by refining an existing one (its superclass). We said that a subclass inherits from a superclass. This way we reuse the code of the superclass instead of rewriting everything from scratch.

Class inheritance creates trees of classes. Such trees are based on *generalisation*: a superclass is more generic than its subclasses. A class in such trees can have instances. All the instances share the behavior defined in their class and superclasses. This is within such trees that the system looks up the method corresponding to a message sent to an instance of a class.

Inheritance supports code reuse because instance variable and methods defined in a root concept (class) are applicable to its refinements (subclasses).

We will use and extend the simple and naive example of files and directories (seen in Chapter 8) to illustrate the key aspects of inheritance. While simple, it is enough to show the key properties of inheritance that we want to illustrate:

- *incremental definition*: a subclass is defined by expressing the difference to its superclass. A subclass specialises its superclass behavior.

- *state reuse*: instances of a subclass have at least the state structure of the superclass.

- *behavior reuse*: upon message reception instances, when the class of the receiver does not define a method, methods of the superclasses are executed instead.

- *behavior redefinition (overriding)*: a subclass may change locally a method definition inherited from its superclass.

- *behavior extension*: a subclass often extends the behavior of one of its superclasses by defining new methods and state.

- *subclass behavior can be invoked instead of superclass behavior*: behavior defined in a subclass may be executed in place of the one of a superclass. It means that with behavior overriding subclass behavior can be invoked in place of superclass behavior. This is a really important feature of inheritance.

14.2 Improving files/directories example design

Let us go back to the example of files and directories introduced in previous chapter. When we look at the situation depicted by Figure 14-1 we see that a file is not the same as a directory, even though they share some common state: both have a name and a parent. In addition, they understand some common messages such as size, search:, parent: and name:. Remember that size and search: were not implemented the same way but the messages have indeed the same name.

Load the code so that you can get the tests that we asked you to define at the end of chapter 8.

```
Gofer new
  smalltalkhubUser: 'StephaneDucasse' project: 'Loop';
  version: 'MyFS2-StephaneDucasse.4';
  load
```

Verify that the tests are all passing (green).

Objectives

In the following sections we will take advantage of defining a common superclass and reuse its definition as shown in Figure 14-2: It means sharing the maximum structure and behavior between the two classes. We will proceed step by step so that you can see all the steps and understand why this is working.

14.3 Transformation strategies

Let us define a new class called MFElement.

```
Object subclass: #MFElement
  instanceVariableNames: ''
  classVariableNames: ''
  package: 'MyFS2'
```

As you may noticed it, this class is empty. Now we have two possible strategies:

- either we make MFFile and MFDirectory inherit from MFElement and step by step we migrate the common state and behavior to the superclass,

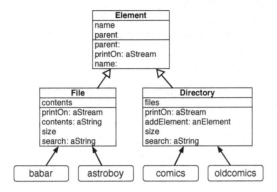

Figure 14-2   Two class taking advantages of inheriting from a common super-class.

- or we define new state and behavior in MFElement and we remove it from the two classes and when ready we make them inherit from MFElement.

The second approach may work but it is too risky. Indeed with the first approach we can get a running system after any step we perform: why? Because we first inherit from the new class and move element from the subclasses to the classes and doing so we automatically reuse the superclass behavior and state so our program externally (for example from the test perspective) is not changed. With such an approach we can run our tests after any change and control our enhancements.

In addition, some of the operations such as moving an instance variable from a class to its superclass are tedious to perform. Here we will perform one operation manually but for the rest of the changes we will use *refactorings* – refactorings are program transformations that keep the behavior of the program the same.

Let us get started.

14.4   **Factoring out state**

The first step is to make MFFile and MFDirectory subclasses of MFElement as follows:

```
MFElement subclass: #MFFile
  instanceVariableNames: 'parent name contents'
  classVariableNames: ''
  package: 'MyFS2'
```

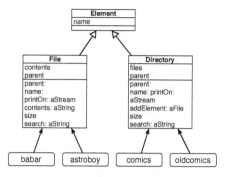

Figure 14-3   Moving the instance variable name to the superclass.

```
MFElement subclass: #MFDirectory
   instanceVariableNames: 'parent name files'
   classVariableNames: ''
   package: 'MyFS2'
```

Now you can execute the tests and they will all pass. Now we get ready move some instance variables to the superclass.

Moving instance variable name to superclass

Since both `MFDirectory` and `MFFile` define that their instances should have a name, we can remove the instance variable name from them and uniquely define it in the superclass. We obtain the situation depicted in Figure 14-3. Let us do that as follows: We remove it first from the `MFFile` and `MFDirectory` classes.

```
MFElement subclass: #MFFile
   instanceVariableNames: 'parent contents'
   classVariableNames: ''
   package: 'MyFS2'
```

```
MFElement subclass: #MFDirectory
   instanceVariableNames: 'parent files'
   classVariableNames: ''
   package: 'MyFS2'
```

And we add the instance variable name to the superclass `MFElement`.

```
Object subclass: #MFElement
   instanceVariableNames: 'name'
   classVariableNames: ''
   package: 'MyFS2'
```

Pay attention that you should be careful and do it in this order else you may be in the situation where name will be defined in the superclass and in one of the subclasses and the system does not allow this and will forbid your action.

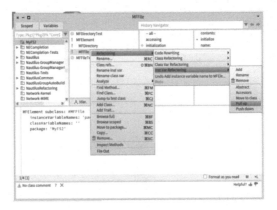

Figure 14-4   Applying the Pull Up Instance variable refactoring.

Again run the tests they should pass again.

What the tests execution proves is that we did not change the structure of the instances of `MFFile` and `MFDirectory`. Indeed the structure of an instance is computed from the instance variable lists defined in their class and all the superclasses of that class.

Moving parent to the superclass

Since parent is defined in both subclasses, we can do the same for the instance variable parent to obtain the situation shown in Figure 14-5. You can do it manually as we did for the instance variable `name` but you can use a *refactoring*: Refactorings are powerful program transformation. Using the system browser, bring the menu on the class `MFFile` select refactoring and select the instance variable category and finally pull up as shown in Figure 14-4.

The system will ask you which variable you want to pull up, select `parent`. It will show you the changes that it is about to perform: removing the instance variable from both subclasses and adding one to the superclass. Proceed and the changes will be executed. Your code should be now in the situation depicted in Figure 14-5. Run the tests and they should again all pass!

What is important to see is that if we create a new subclass of `MFElement`, the instances of such class will automatically get `name` and `parent` as instance variables. This is one of the key property of inheritance: you can define a new abstraction structure by extending an existing one.

Now we can do the same for the behavior: we will move similar methods in the superclass and remove them from their respective classes.

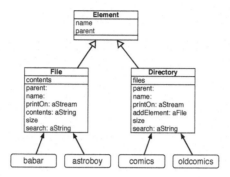

Figure 14-5   State factored between the two classes and their superclass.

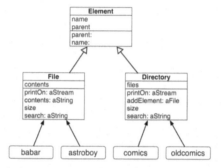

Figure 14-6   State and Methods factored out in the superclass.

14.5   **Factoring similar methods**

The methods parent:, parent and name: are the same and defined in the two classes MFFile and MFDirectory. We will move them to the superclass MFElement following a similar process.

- First we will remove the method name: from the two classes MFFile and MFDirectory and add one version to the class MFElement. You can do this manually.

- Second for the method parent:, use the method Refactoring *Push Up Method* that is available from the method list. You can repeat this for the method parent too.

You should obtain the system described in Figure 14-6.

Again run the tests and they should all pass. Why? Let us see what is happening when we send a message.

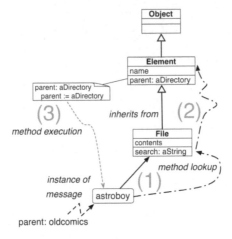

Figure 14-7 When an object receives a message, the corresponding method is looked up in its class and if necessary its superclasses (Step 1 and 2). Then the method is executed on the message receiver (Step 3).

14.6 Sending a message and method lookup

Now it is time to explain what is happening when an object receives a message. In fact this is really simple but extremely powerful. When a message is sent to an object, first the corresponding method is looked up and once the method is found, it is executed on the object that initially received the message.

- **Method Lookup.** When an object, the message receiver, receives a message, the method with the same selector than the message is looked up starting from the *class* of receiver (See step 1 in Figure 14-7). When there is no method with the same selector, the look up continues in the superclass of the current class (See step 2 in Figure 14-7).

- **Method execution.** When a method with the same selector is found in a class, it is returned and executed on the receiver of the message (See step 3 in Figure 14-7).

Let us look at our example.

- When we send the message astroboy parent: oldcomics, the method named parent: is looked up in the class of the receiver i.e., MFFile. This class defines such a method, so it is returned and executed on the file astroboy.

- The tests pass because when we send the message parent: to an instance of the class MFFile, the corresponding method is looked up in the class MFFile. Since there is no method parent: in the class MF-

File, the lookup continues in the superclass and find it in the class MFElement as shown in Figure 14-7.

Inheritance properties

While rather simple, the previous example shows some key properties of inheritance.

Inheritance is a mechanism to define abstraction incrementally: a subclass is defined by expressing the difference to its superclass. A subclass refines a general concept into a more specific one. The classes MFFile and MFDirectory add extra behavior and state to the one defined in the superclass. As such they reuse the state and behavior of their superclass.

- *State reuse*: instances of a subclass have at least the structure of their superclasses (name and parent), local state can be added in addition (contents and files).

- *Behavior reuse*: when instances of a subclass receive a message, methods of the superclass may be executed. The method parent:, parent, and name are defined in MFElement but are executed on instances of the subclasses.

Inheritance creates trees of refined concepts. A superclass represents a more abstract concepts and its subclasses make it more and more specific by refining the superclass behavior or extending it by adding new behavior.

14.7   Basic method overrides

Since the method lookup starts from the class of the receiver, redefining a method in subclass takes precedence over the method defined in the superclasses.

If we define a method with the same name that one of its superclass, this new method will be executed instead of the one in the superclass. This is called a *method override*. This is useful to be able to redefine locally a behavior taking advantage of the specificities of the subclasses. In Figure 14-7, if we add a new method named parent: in the class MFFile, this method will be executed when the message parent: is sent to an instance of the class File.

We will see later that we can also invoke the method of the superclass while doing a method overrides: it is useful when we want to *extend* and not just fully change the superclass behavior.

But before explaining this, method lookup and execution are systematically applied and we will see in the following sections that it is even more powerful than it may look at first sight.

14.8 self-send messages and lookup create hooks

So far we explained how a message is resolved: first the corresponding method is looked up from the class of the receiver and goes up the inheritance tree. Second, the found method is executed on the message receiver. It means that in response to a message, a superclass method may be executed on its subclass instances. This is the same for message sent to self (the receiver of the message), we invoke the method lookup and self may be one subclass instances.

There is an important implication: when we have a message sent to self in a method, this message may lead to the execution of a method defined in subclasses: because a subclass may override such method. This is why self-sends are also called *hooks* methods. We will explain carefully this point.

Example

To explain precisely this important point, let us define a new little behavior: to build a better user interface for end-users we add a new message called describe that presents in more human friendly way the receiver of the message. Here is a small example:

```
| p el1 el2 |
p := MFDirectory new name: 'comics'.
el1 := MFFile new name: 'babar'; contents: 'Babar et Celeste'.
p addElement: el1.
el2 := MFFile new name: 'astroboy'; contents: 'super cool robot'.
p addElement: el2.
p describe
>>> 'I m a directory named comics'
el1 describe
>>> 'I m a file named babar'
```

Describe implementation

We implement now the situation described by Figure 14-8. To implement this behavior, we define the following method describe in the class MFElement.

```
MFElement >> describe
  ^ 'I m a ', self kind, 'named ', name
```

We define the method kind to return a default string, even though we do not expect to create instances of this class and subclasses should define their own definition.

```
MFElement >> kind
  ^ 'element'
```

In each of the subclasses, we define a corresponding method kind, as follows:

```
⎡ MFDirectory >> kind
⎢    ^ 'directory'
⎣
⎡ MFFile >> kind
⎢    ^ 'file'
⎣
```

14.9 **Hook/Template explanations**

Now we are ready to explain what is happening. Let us illustrate the execution of the (MFFile new name: 'astroboy') describe.

```
⎡ | el1 |
⎢ el1 := (MFFile new name: 'astroboy').
⎢ el1 describe
⎣ >>> 'I m a file named astroboy'
```

The following steps are executed:

- The message describe is sent to el1 an instance of the class MFFile.

- The method describe is looked up in the class MFFile (step 1 in Figure 14-8). It is not found, therefore the lookup continues to the superclass.

- The lookup looks for the method describe in the class MFElement (step 2 in Figure 14-8). It is found and executed on the receiver: el1.

- During the execution of the method describe, a new message kind using the expression self kind is sent (step 3 in Figure 14-8).

- The message kind is looked up starting from the class of the receiver, MFFile (step 4 in Figure 14-8). The method kind is found in class MF-FIle and executed.

- The rest of the method describe is executed and the resulting string is returned.

A vocabulary point: the method describe is called a *template* method because it creates a context in which the kind methods are executed. The message kind is called a hook since subclass implementation may be invoked in this place.

This example illustrates the following important points:

- Each time we send a message the system chooses the correct method to be executed.

- Each time we send a self-send message we create a place where subclass methods may be executed. We create customisation points.

- Since self represents the receiver and that the receiver may be an instance from a class that is not loaded at the time the method containing the self-send, we say that self is dynamic. It represents the re-

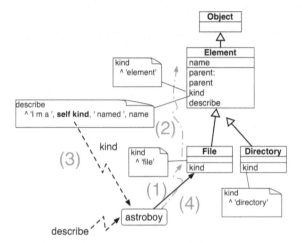

Figure 14-8 A self-send creates a hook (kind) that subclasses override. The method describe is called a template because it creates a context.

ceiver of the message and the lookup for the method to execute starts in the class of the receiver.

Important   Messages sent to the receiver (self sends) define customization points that subclasses can take advantage of to potentially see their code being executed in place of the superclass' one.

14.10   **Essence of self and dispatch**

Now we take some time to look abstractly at what we presented so far. Imagine a situation as illustrated by Figure 14-9.

The first questions are simple and should be not a problem for you. Without looking at the solutions guess what are the results of the following messages.

```
A new foo
>>> ...
B new foo
>>> ...
```

What is more interesting is the process to get the result of B new bar.

```
A new bar
>>> ...
B new bar
>>> ...
```

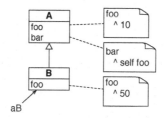

Figure 14-9   Self semantics abstractly explained.

Solutions

The solutions are the following ones.

```
A new foo
>>> 10

B new foo
>>> 50

A new bar
>>> 10

B new bar
>>> 50
```

The most interesting one is B new bar. Let us look at the execution of aB
bar

1. aB's class is B.

2. The method look up starts in the class B.

3. There is no method bar in B.

4. The look up continues in A and method bar is found.

5. The method bar is executed on the receiver aB.

6. self refers to the receiver aB.

7. The message foo is sent to self.

8. The look up of foo starts in the aB's class: B.

9. The method foo is found in class B and executed on the receiver aB.

Important   self represents the receiver. Messages sent to it are looked
up from the class of the receiver.

14.11 Instance variables vs. messages

Reading the previous section you should now understand that there is in fact a difference between accessing directly an instance variable such as name in the method below and using an accessor as illustrated in the next redefinition.

The two following method definitions are doing the same but have different extensibility potential.

```
MFElement >> describe
    ^ 'I m a ', self kind, 'named ', name
```

```
MFElement >> describe
    ^ 'I m a ', self kind, 'named ', self name
```

When you use an accessor, subclasses may redefine the behavior of the accessors.

```
MFElement >> name
    ^ name
```

There is no systematic rule that states that we should systematically use accessors instead of instance variable access.

What is important when you decide to use an accessor is to use it consistently. Indeed if some parts use direct instance variable access and other parts use accessors, then a programmer extending your code may redefine the accessors in a subclass and his code may not be invoked (for example if you left places where you directly access an instance variable).

In addition when you decide to use in your class an accessor it is also better that you do so for all the instance variables of the class. Else we may wonder why and uniformity makes the code more understandable.

14.12 Conclusion

We presented the concept of inheritance: a subclass is defined as a refinement of a superclass. It reuses the superclass behavior and may extend the structure its instances will have. We show that method lookup happens dynamically and walks the inheritance tree starting from the receiver class. We show that self-sends are creating hooks in the sense that subclass methods may be executed in place of the superclass counterpart.

In the following chapter we will see that we can reuse even more methods between all the superclass and its subclasses.

15

Extending superclass behavior

In the previous chapter we saw that inheritance allows the programmer to factor out and reuse state and behavior. As such inheritance supports the definition of class hierarchy where subclasses specialize behavior of their superclass. We saw that the method look up starts in the class of the receiver and goes up the inheritance chain. We explained that the method found by the lookup is then executed on the receiver of the initial message. Finally we showed that a subclass can specialize and override the behavior of its superclass by defining locally a method with the same name than one method of its superclass.

Now inheritance mechanism is even more powerful. With inheritance we can extend locally the behavior of a superclass while reusing it. It is then possible to override a method and in addition to invoke the behavior of the superclass from within the overridden method.

We will continue to use and improve the example of file and directories.

15.1 **Revisiting printOn:**

When we look at the following printOn: methods defined in the classes MFDirectory and MFFile we see that there is code repetition (as shown in Figure 15-1).

Here is the repeated code snippet.

```
parent isNil
   ifFalse: [ parent printOn: aStream ].
aStream << name
```

Here is the definition in the two classes:

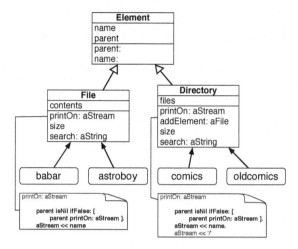

Figure 15-1 `MFFile` and `MFDirectory` contain duplicated logic in `printOn:`.

```
MFDirectory >> printOn: aStream
  parent isNil
    ifFalse: [ parent printOn: aStream ].
  aStream << name.
  aStream << '/'

MFFile >> printOn: aStream
  parent isNil
    ifFalse: [ parent printOn: aStream ].
  aStream << name
```

It means that if we define a new subclass we will have probably duplicate the same expression.

15.2 Improving the situation

To improve the situation above we move up the definition of the `MFFile` class because it also works for `MFElement` (as shown in Figure 15-2).

```
MFElement >> printOn: aStream
  parent isNil
    ifFalse: [ parent printOn: aStream ].
  aStream << name

MFDirectory >> printOn: aStream
  parent isNil
    ifFalse: [ parent printOn: aStream ].
  aStream << name.
  aStream << '/'
```

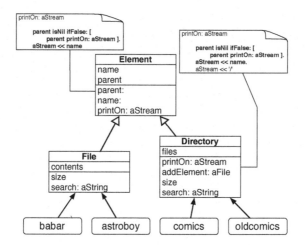

Figure 15-2 Improving the logic (but not fully).

It means that when we will add a new subclass, this class will at least have a default definition for the `printOn:` method.

Now the duplication of logic is not addressed. The same code is duplicated between the class `MFElement` and `MFDirectory`. What we see is that even if the method `printOn:` of class `MFDirectory` is overriding the method of its superclass, we would like to be able to invoke the method of the superclass `MFElement` and to add the behavior `aStream << '/'`.

Why self does not work!

The following definition does not work because it introduces an endless loop. Indeed, since the method lookup starts in the class of the receiver and `self` represents the receiver, it will always find the same method and will not be able to access the method of the superclass.

```
MFDirectory >> printOn: aStream
  self printOn: aStream.
  aStream << '/'
```

Let us make sure that you are fully with us. Imagine that we have the following expression:

```
| p el1 el2 |
p := MFDirectory new name: 'comics'.
el1 := MFFile new name: 'babar'; contents: 'Babar et Celeste'.
p addElement: el1.
el2 := MFFile new name: 'astroboy'; contents: 'super cool robot'.
p addElement: el2.
String streamContents: [:s | p printOn: s ]
```

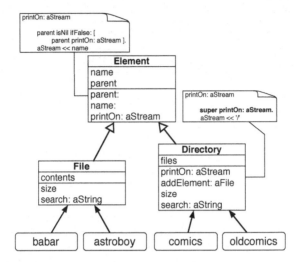

Figure 15-3 Using super to invoke the overridden method printOn:.

1. We get the message p printOn: s.

2. The method printOn: is looked up starting in the class of p, i.e., MFDirectory.

3. The method is found and applied on p.

4. The message self printOn: aStream is about to be executed.

5. The receiver is self and represents p. The method printOn: aStream is looked up in the class of the receiver, i.e., MFDirectory.

6. The same method is found in the class MFDirectory and the process restarts at point 3.

In summary, we would like that while doing an override, to use the behavior we are overriding. This is possible as we will see in the following section.

15.3 Extending superclass behavior using super

Let us implement the solution first and discuss it after. We redefine the method printOn: of the class MFDirectory as follows and shown in Figure 15-3.

```
MFDirectory >> printOn: aStream
  super printOn: aStream.
  aStream << '/'
```

What we see is that the method printOn: does not contain anymore the duplicated expressions with the method printOn: of the superclass (MFElement). Instead by using the special variable super the superclass method is invoked. Let us look at it in detail.

- The method MFDirectory >> printOn: overrides the method MFElement: it means that during the lookup (activated because the message
  printOn: has been sent to instances of MFDirectory or future subclasses), the method MFElement >> printOn: cannot be directly
  found. Indeed when a message is sent to an object, the corresponding method starts in the class of the receiver, therefore the method in
  MFDirectory is found.

- Using the special variable super, the method lookup is different than
  with self. When the expression super printOn: aStream is sent, the
  lookup does not start anymore from the class of the receiver, it starts
  from the superclass of the class containing the expression super printOn:,
  i.e. MFElement, therefore the method of the superclass is found and
  executed.

- Finally, super like self represents the receiver of the messages (for
  example an instance of the class MFDirectory). Therefore the method
  is found in the class MFDirectory and executed on the original object
  that first received the message.

Let us make sure that you are fully with us. You can compare with the previous execution simulation.

```
| p el1 el2 |
p := MFDirectory new name: 'comics'.
el1 := MFFile new name: 'babar'; contents: 'Babar et Celeste'.
p addElement: el1.
el2 := MFFile new name: 'astroboy'; contents: 'super cool robot'.
p addElement: el2.
String streamContents: [:s | p printOn: s ]
```

1. We get the message p printOn: s.

2. The method printOn: is looked up starting in the class of p, i.e., MFDirectory.

3. The method is found and applied on p.

4. The message super printOn: aStream is about to be executed.

5. The receiver is super and represents p. The method printOn: aS-
   tream is looked up in the superclass of the class containing the expression. The class containing the method is MFDirectory, its superclass is
   then MFElement. The lookup starts from MFElement.

6. The method is found in the class MFElement in the class.

7. The message parent isNil is treated on the receiver p.

What we see is that using super, the programmer can extend the superclass
behavior and reuse by involving it.

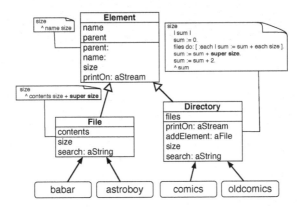

Figure 15-4 Using super to invoke the overridden method size.

> **Important**   super is the receiver of the message but when we send a
> message to super the method lookup starts in the superclass of **the class**
> **containing** the expression super.

15.4 **Another example**

Before explaining with a more theoritical scenario *super* semantics, we want
to show another example that illustrates that super expressions do not have
to be the first expression of a method. We can invoke the overridden method
at any place inside the overriding method.

The example could be more realistic but it shows that super expression does
not have to have to be the first expression of a method.

Let us check the two definitions of the two methods size in MFDirectory
and MFFile, we see that name size is used in both.

```
MFDirectory >> size
  | sum |
  sum := 0.
  files do: [ :each | sum := sum + each size ].
  sum := sum + name size.
  sum := sum + 2.
  ^ sum
```
```
MFFile >> size
  ^ contents size + name size
```

What we can do is the following: define size in the superclass and invoke it
using super as shown in Figure 15-4. Here is then the resulting situation.

```
MFElement >> size
  ^ name size
```

```
MFFile >> size
   ^ contents size + super size
```

```
MFDirectory >> size
   | sum |
   sum := 0.
   files do: [ :each | sum := sum + each size ].
   sum := sum + super size.
   sum := sum + 2.
   ^ sum
```

What you see is that messages sent to super can be used anywhere inside in the overriding method and their results can be used as any other messages.

15.5   Really understanding super

To convince you that self and super points to the same object you can use the message == to verify it as follows:

```
MFFile >> funky
   ^ super == self
```

```
MFFile new funky
>>> true
```

> **Important**   super is a special variable: super (just like self) is the receiver of the message!

Now we take some time to look abstractly at what we presented so far. Imagine a situation as illustrated by Figure 15-5.

```
A new bar
>>> ...
C new bar
>>> ...
D new bar
>>> ...
```

Solution

The solutions are the following ones:

```
A new bar
>>> 10
C new bar
>>> 20
D new bar
>>> 100
```

Let us examine the evaluation of the message aD bar:

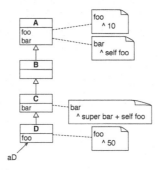

Figure 15-5 Example to understand `super`.

1. aD's class is D.

2. There is no method `bar` in D.

3. The method look up in C. The method `bar` is found.

4. The method `bar` of C is executed.

5. The message `bar` is sent to `super`.

6. `super` represents aD but the lookup starts in the superclass of the class containing the expression `super` so it starts in B.

7. The method `bar` is not found in B, the lookup continues in A.

8. The method `bar` is found in A and it is executed on the receiver i.e., aD.

9. The message `foo` is sent to aD.

10. The method `foo` is found in D and executed. It returns 50.

11. Then to finish the execution of method `bar` in C, the rest of the expression + `self foo` should be executed.

12. Message `self foo` returns 50 too, so the result returns 100.

> **Important**   The difference between `self` and `super` is that when we send a message to `super` the method lookup starts in the superclass of the class containing the expression `super`.

15.6 Conclusion

In this chapter we saw that inheritance also supports the possibilities to override a method and from this overriding method to invoke the overridden one. This is done using the special variable `super`. `super` is the receiver of the message like `self`. The difference is that the method lookup is changed when messages are sent to `super`. The method is looked up in the superclass of the class containing the message sent to `super`.

16

A little expression interpreter

In this chapter you will build a small mathematical expression interpreter. For example you will be able to build an expression such as (3 + 4) * 5 and then ask the interpreter to compute its value. You will revisit tests, classes, messages, methods and inheritance. You will also see an example of expression trees similar to the ones that are used to manipulate programs. For example, compilers and code refactorings as offered in Pharo and many modern IDEs are doing such manipulation with trees representing code. In addition, in the volume two of this book, we will extend this example to present the Visitor Design Pattern.

16.1 Starting with constant expression and a test

We start with constant expression. A constant expression is an expression whose value is always the same, obviously.

Let us start by defining a test case class as follows:

```
TestCase subclass: #EConstantTest
  instanceVariableNames: ''
  classVariableNames: ''
  package: 'Expressions'
```

We decided to define one test case class per expression class and this even if at the beginning the classes will not contain many tests. It is easier to define new tests and navigate them.

Let us write a first test making sure that when we get a value, sending it the evaluate message returns its value.

```
EConstantTest >> testEvaluate
  self assert: (EConstant new value: 5) evaluate equals: 5
```

When you compile such a test method, the system should prompt you to get a class EConstant defined. Let the system drive you. Since we need to store the value of a constant expression, let us add an instance variable value to the class definition.

At the end you should have the following definition for the class EConstant.

```
Object subclass: #EConstant
  instanceVariableNames: 'value'
  classVariableNames: ''
  package: 'Expressions'
```

We define the method value: to set the value of the instance variable value. It is simply a method taking one argument and storing it in the value instance variable.

```
EConstant >> value: anInteger
  value := anInteger
```

You should define the method evaluate: it should return the value of the constant.

```
EConstant >> evaluate
  ... Your code ...
```

Your test should pass.

16.2 Negation

Now we can start to work on expression negation. Let us write a test and for this define a new test case class named ENegationTest.

```
TestCase subclass: #ENegationTest
  instanceVariableNames: ''
  classVariableNames: ''
  package: 'Expressions'
```

The test testEvaluate shows that a negation applies to an expression (here a constant) and when we evalute we get the negated value of the constant.

```
ENegationTest >> testEvaluate
  self assert: (ENegation new expression: (EConstant new value: 5))
    evaluate equals: -5
```

Let us execute the test and let the system help us to define the class. A negation defines an instance variable to hold the expression that it negates.

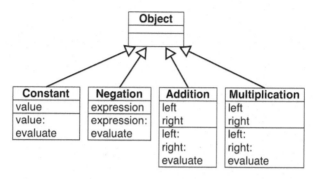

Figure 16-1   A flat collection of classes (with a suspect duplication).

```
Object subclass: #ENegation
  instanceVariableNames: 'expression'
  classVariableNames: ''
  package: 'Expressions'
```

We define a setter method to be able to set the expression under negation.

```
ENegation >> expression: anExpression
  expression := anExpression
```

Now the evaluate method should request the evaluation of the expression and negate it. To negate a number the Pharo library proposes the message negated.

```
ENegation >> evaluate
  ... Your code ...
```

Following the same principle, we will add expression addition and multiplication. Then we will make the system a bit more easy to manipulate and revisit its first design.

16.3   Adding expression addition

To be able to do more than constant and negation we will add two extra expressions: addition and multiplication and after we will discuss about our approach and see how we can improve it.

To add an expression that supports addition, we start to define a test case class and a simple test.

```
TestCase subclass: #EAdditionTest
  instanceVariableNames: ''
  classVariableNames: ''
  package: 'Expressions'
```

A simple test for addition is to make sure that we add correctly two constants.

```
EAdditionTest >> testEvaluate
  | ep1 ep2 |
  ep1 := (EConstant new value: 5).
  ep2 := (EConstant new value: 3).
  self assert: (EAddition new right: ep1; left: ep2) evaluate
    equals: 8
```

You should define the class EAddition: it has two instance variables for the two subexpressions it adds.

```
EExpression subclass: #EAddition
  instanceVariableNames: 'left right'
  classVariableNames: ''
  package: 'Expressions'
```

Define the two corresponding setter methods right: and left:.

Now you can define the evaluate method for addition.

```
EAddition >> evaluate
  ... Your code ...
```

To make sure that our implementation is correct we can also test that we can add negated expressions. It is always good to add tests that cover *different* scenario.

```
EAdditionTest >> testEvaluateWithNegation
  | ep1 ep2 |
  ep1 := ENegation new expression: (EConstant new value: 5).
  ep2 := (EConstant new value: 3).
  self assert: (EAddition new right: ep1; left: ep2) evaluate
    equals: -2
```

16.4 Multiplication

We do the same for multiplication: create a test case class named EMultiplicationTest, a test, a new class EMultiplication, a couple of setter methods and finally a new evaluate method. Let us do it fast and without much comments.

```
TestCase subclass: #EMultiplicationTest
  instanceVariableNames: ''
  classVariableNames: ''
  package: 'Expressions'
```

```
EMultiplicationTest >> testEvaluate
  | ep1 ep2 |
  ep1 := (EConstant new value: 5).
  ep2 := (EConstant new value: 3).
```

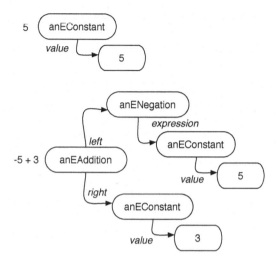

Figure 16-2 Expressions are composed of trees.

```
self assert: (EMultiplication new right: ep1; left: ep2) evaluate
    equals: 15
```

```
Object subclass: #EMultiplication
  instanceVariableNames: 'left right'
  classVariableNames: ''
  package: 'Expressions'
```

```
EMultiplication >> right: anExpression
  right := anExpression
```

```
EMultiplication >> left: anExpression
  left := anExpression
```

```
EMultiplication >> evaluate
  ... Your code ...
```

16.5 Stepping back

It is interesting to look at what we built so far. We have a group of classes whose instances can be combined to create complex expressions. Each expression is in fact a tree of subexpressions as shown in Figure 16-2. The figure shows two main trees: one for the constant expression 5 and one for the expression -5 + 3. Note that the diagram represents the number 5 as an object because in Pharo even small integers are objects in the same way the instances of EConstant are objects.

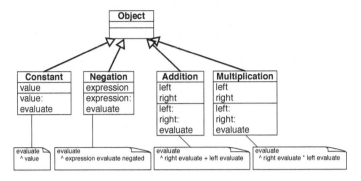

Figure 16-3 Evaluation: one message and multiple method implementations.

Messages and methods

The implementation of the evaluate message is worth discussing. What we see is that *different* classes understand the same message but execute different methods as shown in Figure 16-3.

> **Important** A message represents an intent: it represents *what* should be done. A method represents a specification of *how* something should be executed.

What we see is that sending a message evaluate to an expression is making a choice among the different implementations of the message. This point is central to object-oriented programming.

> **Important** Sending a message is making a choice among all the methods with the same name.

About common superclass

So far we did not see the need to have an inheritance hierarchy because there is not much to share or reuse. Now adding a common superclass would be useful to convey to the reader of the code or a future extender of the library that such concepts are related and are different variations of expression.

Design corner: About addition and multiplication model

We could have just one class called for example BinaryOperation and it can have an operator and this operator will be either the addition or multiplication. This solution can work and as usual having a working program does not mean that its design is any good.

In particular having a single class would force us to start to write conditional based on the operator as follows

```
BinaryExpression >> evaluate
  operator = #+
    ifTrue: [ left evaluate + right evaluate ]
    ifFalse: [ left evaluate * right evaluate]
```

There are ways in Pharo to make such code more compact but we do not want to use it at this stage. For the interested reader, look for the message perform: that can execute a method based on its name.

This is annoying because the execution engine itself is made to select methods for us so we want to avoid to bypass it using explicit condition. In addition when we will add power, division, subtraction we will have to have more cases in our condition making the code less readable and more fragile.

As we will see as a general message in this book, sending a message is making a choice between different implementations. Now to be able to choose we should have different implementations and this implies having different classes.

Important   Classes represent choices whose methods can be selected in reaction to a message. Having many little classes is better than few large ones.

What we could do is to introduce a common superclass between EAddition and EMultiplication but keep the two subclasses. We will probably do it in the future

16.6   **Negated as a message**

Negating an expression is expressed in a verbose way. We have to create explicitly each time an instance of the class ENegation as shown in the following snippet.

```
ENegation new expression: (EConstant new value: 5)
```

We propose to define a message negated on the expressions themselves that will create such instance of ENegation. With this new message, the previous expression can be reduced too.

```
(EConstant new value: 5) negated
```

negated message for constants

Let us write a test to make sure that we capture well what we want to get.

```
EConstantTest >> testNegated
  self assert: (EConstant new value: 6) negated evaluate equals: -6
```

And now we can simply implement it as follows:

```
EConstant >> negated
  ^ ENegation new expression: self
```

negated message for negations

```
ENegationTest >> testNegationNegated
  self assert: (EConstant new value: 6) negated negated evaluate
    equals: 6
```

```
ENegation >> negated
  ^ ENegation new expression: self
```

This definition is not the best we can do since in general it is a bad practice to hardcode the class usage inside the class. A better definition would be

```
ENegation >> negated
  ^ self class new expression: self
```

But for now we keep the first one for the sake of simplicity

negated message for additions

We proceed similarly for additions.

```
EEAdditionTest >> testNegated
  | ep1 ep2 |
  ep1 := EConstant new value: 5.
  ep2 := EConstant new value: 3.
  self assert: (EAddition new right: ep1; left: ep2) negated
    evaluate equals: -8
```

```
EAddition >> negated
  Your code
```

negated message for multiplications

We proceed similarly for multiplications.

```
EMultiplicationTest >> testEvaluateNegated
  | ep1 ep2 |
  ep1 := EConstant new value: 5.
  ep2 := EConstant new value: 3.
  self assert: (EMultiplication new right: ep1; left: ep2) negated
    evaluate equals: -15
```

```
EMultiplication >> negated
  ... Your code ...
```

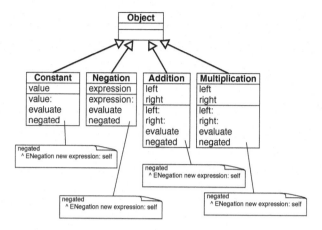

Figure 16-4 Code repetition is a bad smell.

Now all your tests should pass. And it is a good moment to save your package.

16.7 **Annoying repetition**

Let us step back and look at what we have. We have a working situation but again object-oriented design is to bring the code to a better level.

Similarly to the situation of the evaluate message and methods we see that the functionality of negated is distributed over different classes. Now what is annoying is that we repeat the exact *same* code over and over and this is not good (see Figure 16-4). This is not good because if tomorrow we want to change the behavior of negation we will have to change it four times while in fact one time should be enough.

What are the solutions?

- We could define another class Negator that would do the job and each current classes would delegate to it. But it does not really solve our problem since we will have to duplicate all the message sends to call Negator instances.

- If we define the method negated in the superclass (Object) we only need one definition and it will work. Indeed, when we send the message negated to an instance of EConstant or EAddition the system will not find it locally but in the superclass Object. So no need to define it four times but only one in class Object. This solution is nice because it reduces the number of similar definitions of the method negated but it is not good because even if in Pharo we can add methods to the class Object this is not a good practice. Object is a class

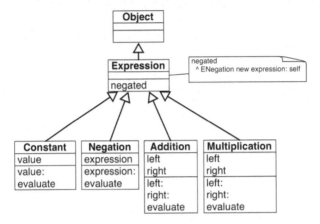

Figure 16-5 Introducing a common superclass.

shared by the entire system so we should take care not to add behavior only making sense for a single application.

- The solution is to introduce a new superclass between our classes and the class Object. It will have the same property than the solution with Object but without polluting it (see Figure 16-5). This is what we do in the next section.

16.8 Introducing Expression class

Let us introduce a new class to obtain the situation depicted by Figure 16-5. We can simply do it by adding a new class:

```
Object subclass: #EExpression
    instanceVariableNames: ''
    classVariableNames: ''
    package: 'Expressions'
```

and changing all the previous definitions to inherit from EExpression instead of Object. For example the class EConstant is then defined as follows.

```
EExpression subclass: #EConstant
    instanceVariableNames: 'value'
    classVariableNames: ''
    package: 'Expressions'
```

We can also use for the first transformation the class refactoring *Insert superclass*. Refactorings are code transformations that do not change the behavior of a program. You can find it under the refactorings list when you bring the menu on the classes. Now it is only useful for the first changes.

Once the classes `EConstant`, `ENegation`, `EAddition`, and `EMultiplication` are subclasses of `EEXpression`, we should focus on the method `negated`. Now the method refactoring *Push up* will really help us.

- Select the method `negated` in one of the classes
- Select the refactoring *Push up*

The system will define the method `negated` in the superclass (`EExpression`) and remove all the negated methods in the classes. Now we obtain the situation described in Figure 16-5. It is a good moment to run all your tests again. They should all pass.

Now you could think that we can introduce a new class named Arithmetic-Expression as a superclass of `EAddition` and `EMultiplication`. Indeed this is something that we could do to factor out common structure and behavior between the two classes. We will do it later because this is basically just a repetition of what we have done.

16.9 Class creation messages

Until now we always sent the message new to a class followed by a setter method as shown below.

```
EConstant new value: 5
```

We would like to take the opportunity to show that we can define simple **class** methods to improve the class instance creation interface. In this example it is simple and the benefits are not that important but we think that this is a nice example. With this in mind the previous example can now be written as follows:

```
EConstant value: 5
```

Notice the important difference that in the first case the message is sent to the newly created instance while in the second case it is sent to the class itself.

To define a class method is the same as to define an instance method (as we did until now). The only difference is that using the code browser you should click on the classSide button to indicate that you are defining a method that should be executed in response to a message sent to a class itself.

Better instance creation for constants

Define the following method on the class `EConstant`. Notice the definition now use `EConstant class` and not just `EConstant` to stress that we are defining the class method.

```
EConstant class >> value: anInteger
   ^ self new value: anInteger
```

Now define a new test to make sure that our method works correctly.

```
EConstantTest >> testCreationWithClassCreationMessage
  self assert: (EConstant value: 5) evaluate equals: 5
```

Better instance creation for negations

We do the same for the class ENegation.

```
ENegation class >> expression: anExpression
   ... Your code ...
```

We write of course a new test as follows:

```
ENegationTest >> testEvaluateWithClassCreationMessage
  self assert: (ENegation expression: (EConstant value: 5)) evaluate
    equals: -5
```

Better instance creation for additions

For the addition we add a class method named left:right: taking two arguments

```
EAddition class >> left: anInteger right: anInteger2
   ^ self new left: anInteger ; right: anInteger2
```

Of course, since we are addicted to tests, we add a new test.

```
EEAdditionTest >> testEvaluateWithClassCreationMessage
  | ep1 ep2 |
  ep1 := EConstant constant5.
  ep2 := EConstant constant3.
  self assert: (EAddition left: ep1 right: ep2) evaluate equals: 8
```

Better instance creation for multiplications

We let you do the same for the multiplication.

```
EMultiplication class >> left: anExp right: anExp2
   ... Your code ...
```

And another test to check that everything is ok.

```
EMultiplicationTest >> testEvaluateWithClassCreationMessage
  | ep1 ep2 |
  ep1 := EConstant new value: 5.
  ep2 := EConstant new value: 3.
  self assert: (EMultiplication new left: ep1; right: ep2) evaluate
    equals: 15
```

Run your tests! They should all pass.

16.10 Introducing examples as class messages

As you saw when writing the tests, it is quite annoying to repeat all the time the expressions to get a given tree. This is especially the case in the tests related to addition and multiplication as the one below:

```
EEAdditionTest >> testNegated
  | ep1 ep2 |
  ep1 := EConstant new value: 5.
  ep2 := EConstant new value: 3.
  self assert: (EAddition new right: ep1; left: ep2) negated
    evaluate equals: -8
```

One simple solution is to define some class methods returning typical instances of their classes. To define a class method remember that you should click the class side button.

```
EConstant class >> constant5
  ^ self new value: 5
```

```
EConstant class >> constant3
  ^ self new value: 3
```

This way we can define the test as follows:

```
EEAdditionTest >> testNegated
  | ep1 ep2 |
  ep1 := EConstant constant5.
  ep2 := EConstant constant3.
  self assert: (EAddition new right: ep1; left: ep2) negated
    evaluate equals: -8
```

The tools in Pharo support such a practice. If we tag a class method with the special annotation <sampleInstance> the browser will show a little icon on the side and when we click on it, it will open an inspector on the new instance.

```
EConstant class >> constant3
  <sampleInstance>
  ^ self new value: 3
```

using the same idea we defined the following class methods to return some examples of our classes.

```
EAddition class >> fivePlusThree
  <sampleInstance>
  | ep1 ep2 |
  ep1 := EConstant new value: 5.
  ep2 := EConstant new value: 3.
  ^ self new left: ep1 ; right: ep2
```

```
EMultiplication class >> fiveTimesThree
  <sampleInstance>
  | ep1 ep2 |
  ep1 := EConstant constant5.
  ep2 := EConstant constant3.
  ^ EMultiplication new left: ep1 ; right: ep2
```

What is nice with such examples is that

- they help documenting the class by providing objects that we can directly use,

- they support the creation of tests by providing objects that can serve as input for tests,

- they simplify the writing of tests.

So think to use them.

16.11 Printing

It is quite annoying that we cannot really see an expression when we inspect it. We would like to get something better than 'aEConstant' and 'anEAddition' when we debug our programs. To display such information the debugger and inspector send to the objects the message printString which by default just prefix the name of the class with 'an' or 'a'.

Let us change this situation. For this, we will specialize the method printOn: aStream. The message printOn: is called on the object when a program or the system send to the object the message printString. From that perspective printOn: is a system customisation point that developers can take advantage to enhance their programming experience.

Note that we do not redefine the method printString because it is more complex and printString is reused for all the objects in the system. We just have to implement the part that is specific to a given class. In object-oriented design jargon, printString is a template method in the sense that it sets up a context which is shared by other objects and it hosts hook methods which are program customisation points. printOn: is a hook method. The term hook comes from the fact that code of subclasses are invoked in the hook place (see Figure 16-6).

The default definition of the method printOn: as defined on the class Object is the following: it grabs the class name and checks if it starts with a vowel or not and write to the stream the 'a/an class'. This is why by default we got 'anEConstant' when we printed a constant expression.

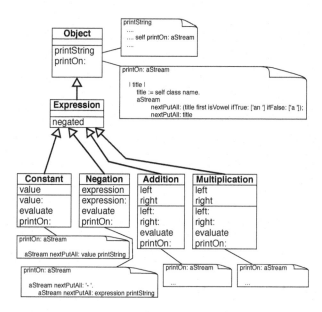

Figure 16-6 printOn: and printString a "hooks and template" in action.

```
Object >> printOn: aStream
  "Append to the argument, aStream, a sequence of characters that
  identifies the receiver."
  | title |
  title := self class name.
  aStream
    nextPutAll: (title first isVowel ifTrue: ['an '] ifFalse: ['a
    ']);
    nextPutAll: title
```

A word about streams

A stream is basically a container for a sequence of objects. Once we get a stream we can either read from it or write to it. In our case we will write to the stream. Since the stream passed to printOn: is a stream expecting characters we will add characters or strings (sequence of characters) to it. We will use the messages: nextPut: aCharacter and nextPutAll: aString. They add to the stream the arguments at the next position and following. We will guide you and it is simple. You can find more information on the chapter about Stream in the book: Pharo by Example available at http://books.pharo.org

Printing constant

Let us start with a test. Here we check that a constant is printed as its value.

```
EConstantTest >> testPrinting
  self assert: (EConstant value: 5) printString equals: '5'
```

The implementation is then simple. We just need to put the value converted as a string to the stream.

```
EConstant >> printOn: aStream
  aStream nextPutAll: value printString
```

Printing negation

For a negation we should first put a '-' and then recursively call the printing process on the negated expression. Remember that sending the message printString to an expression should return its string representation. At least until now it will work for constants.

```
(EConstant value: 6) printString
>>> '6'
```

Here is a possible definition

```
ENegation >> printOn: aStream
  aStream nextPutAll: '- '
  aStream nextPutAll: expression printString
```

By the way since all the messages are sent to the same object, this method can be rewritten as:

```
ENegation >> printOn: aStream
  aStream
    nextPutAll: '- ';
    nextPutAll: expression printString
```

We can also define it as follows:

```
ENegation >> printOn: aStream
  aStream nextPutAll: '- '.
  expression printOn: aStream
```

The difference between the first solution and the alternate implementation is the following: In the solution using printString, the system creates two streams: one for each invocation of the message printString. One for printing the expression and one for printing the negation. Once the first stream is used the message printString converts the stream contents into a string and this new string is put inside the second stream which at the end is converted again as a string. So the first solution is not really efficient. With the second solution, only one stream is created and each of the method just put the needed string elements inside. At the end of the process, the single printString message converts it into a string.

Printing addition

Now let us write yet another test for addition printing.

```
EAdditionTest >> testPrinting
    self assert: (EAddition fivePlusThree) printString equals: '( 5 +
        3 )'.
    self assert: (EAddition fivePlusThree) negated printString equals:
        '- ( 5 + 3 )'
```

Printing an addition is: put an open parenthesis, print the left expression, put '+', print the right expression and put a closing parenthesis in the stream.

```
EAddition >> printOn: aStream
    ... Your code ...
```

Printing multiplication

And now we do the same for multiplication.

```
EMultiplicationTest >> testPrinting
    self assert: (EMultiplication fiveTimesThree) negated printString
        equals: '- ( 5 * 3 )'
```

```
EMultiplication >> printOn: aStream
    ... Your code ...
```

16.12 Revisiting negated message for Negation

Now we can go back on negating an expression. Our implementation is not nice even if we can negate any expression and get the correct value. If you look at it carefully negating a negation could be better. Printing a negated negation illustrates well the problem: we get two minuses instead of none.

```
(EConstant value: 11) negated
>> '- 11'

(EConstant value: 11) negated negated
>> '- - 11'
```

A solution could be to change the printOn: definition and to check if the expression that is negated is a negation and in such case to not emit the minus. Let us say it now, this solution is not nice because we do not want to write code that depends on explicitly checking if an object is of a given class. Remember we want to send message and let the object do some actions.

A good solution is to *specialize* the message negated so that when it is sent to a *negation* it does not create a new negation that points to the receiver but instead returns the expression itself, otherwise the method implemented in

EExpression will be executed. This way the trees created by a negated message can never have negated negation but the arithmetic values obtained are correct. Let us implement this solution, we just need to implement a different version of the method negated for ENegation.

Let us write a test! Since evaluating a single expression or a double negated one gives the same results, we need to define a structural test. This is what we do with the expression exp negated class = ENegation below.

```
NegationTest >> testNegatedStructureIsCorrect
  | exp |
  exp := EConstant value: 11.
  self assert: exp negated class = ENegation.
  self assert: exp negated negated equals: exp.
```

Now you should be able to implement the negated message on ENegation.

```
ENegation >> negated
  ... Your code ...
```

Understanding method override

When we send a message to an object, the system looks for the corresponding method in the class of the receiver then if it is not defined there, the lookup continues in the superclass of the previous class.

By adding a method in the class ENegation, we created the situation shown in Figure 16-7. We said that the message negated is overridden in ENegation because for instances of ENegation it hides the method defined in the superclass EExpression.

It works the following:

- When we send the message negated to a constant, the message is not found in the class EConstant and then it is looked up in the class EExpression and it is found there and applied to the receiver (the instance of EConstant).

- When we send the message negated to a negation, the message is found in the class ENegation and executed on the negation expression.

16.13 Introducing BinaryExpression class

Now we will take a moment to improve our first design. We will factor out the behavior of EAddition and EMultiplication.

```
EExpression subclass: #EBinaryExpression
  instanceVariableNames: ''
  classVariableNames: ''
  package: 'Expressions'
```

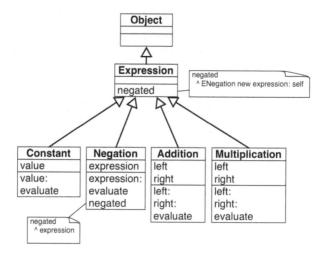

Figure 16-7   The message `negated` is overridden in the class `ENegation`.

```
EBinaryExpression subclass: #EAddition
  instanceVariableNames: 'left right'
  classVariableNames: ''
  package: 'Expressions'
```

```
EBinaryExpression subclass: #EMultiplication
  instanceVariableNames: 'left right'
  classVariableNames: ''
  package: 'Expressions'
```

Now we can use again a refactoring to pull up the instance variables `left` and `right`, as well as the methods `left:` and `right:`.

Select the class `EMuplication`, bring the menu and select in the Refactoring menu the instance variables refactoring *Push Up*. Then select the instance variables.

Now you should get the following class definitions, where the instance variables are defined in the new class and removed from the two subclasses.

```
EExpression subclass: #EBinaryExpression
  instanceVariableNames: 'left right'
  classVariableNames: ''
  package: 'Expressions'
```

```
EBinaryExpression subclass: #EAddition
  instanceVariableNames: ''
  classVariableNames: ''
  package: 'Expressions'
```

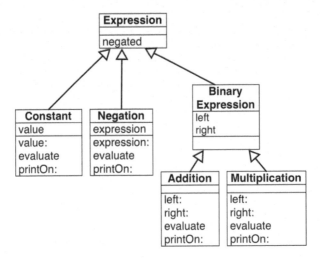

Figure 16-8 Factoring instance variables.

```
EBinaryExpression subclass: #EMultiplication
  instanceVariableNames: ''
  classVariableNames: ''
  package: 'Expressions'
```

We should get a situation similar to the one of Figure 16-8. All your tests should still pass.

Now we can move the same way the methods. Select the method `left:` and apply the refactoring *Pull Up Method*. Do the same for the method `right:`.

Creating a template and hook method

Now we can look at the methods `printOn:` of additions and multiplications. They are really similar: Just the operator is changing. Now we cannot simply copy one of the definitions because it will not work for the other. But what we can do is to apply the same design point that implemented for `printString` and `printOn::` we can create a template and hooks that will be specialized in the subclasses.

We will use the method `printOn:` as a template with a hook redefined in each subclass.

Let define the method `printOn:` in `EBinaryExpression` and remove the other ones from the two classes `EAddition` and `EMultiplication`.

```
EBinaryExpression >> printOn: aStream
  aStream nextPutAll: '( '.
  left printOn: aStream.
  aStream nextPutAll: ' + '.
```

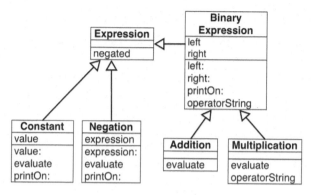

Figure 16-9   Factoring instance variables and behavior.

```
  right printOn: aStream.
  aStream nextPutAll: ' )'
```

Then you can do it manually or use the *Extract Method* Refactoring: This refactoring creates a new method from a part of an existing method and sends a message to the new created method: select the ' + ' inside the method pane and bring the menu and select the Extract Method refactoring, and when prompt give the name operatorString.

Here is the result you should get:

```
EBinaryExpression >> printOn: aStream
  aStream nextPutAll: '( '.
  left printOn: aStream.
  aStream nextPutAll: self operatorString.
  right printOn: aStream.
  aStream nextPutAll: ' )'
```

```
EBinaryExpression >> operatorString
  ^ ' + '
```

Now we can just redefine this method in the EMultiplication class to return the adequate string.

```
EMultiplication >> operatorString
  ^ ' * '
```

16.14   **What did we learn**

The introduction of the class EBinaryExpression is a rich experience in terms of lessons that we can learn.

- Refactorings are more than simple code transformations. Usually refactorings pay attention that their application does not change the behavior of programs. As we saw refactorings are powerful operations that really help doing complex operations in a few action.

- We saw that the introduction of a new superclass and moving instance variables or method to a superclass does not change the structure or behavior of the subclasses. This is because (1) for the state, the structure of an instance is based on the state of its class and all its superclasses, (2) the lookup starts in the class of the receiver and look in superclasses.

- While the method printOn: is by itself a hook for the method printString, it can also play the role of a template method. The method operatorString reuses the context created by the printOn: method which acts as a template method. In fact each time we do a self send we create a hook method that subclasses can specialize.

16.15 About hook methods

When we introduced EBinaryExpression we defined the method operatorString as follows:

```
EBinaryExpression >> operatorString
    ^ ' + '
```

```
EMultiplication >> operatorString
    ^ ' * '
```

And you may wonder if it was worth to create a new method in the superclass and so that such one subclass redefines it.

Creating hooks is always good

First creating a hook is also a good idea. Because you rarely know how your system will be extended in the future. On this little example, we suggest you to add raising to power, division and this can be done with one class and two methods per new operator.

Avoid not documenting hooks

Second we could have just defined one method operatorString in each subclass and no method in the superclass EBinaryExpression. It would have worked because EBinaryExpression is not meant to have direct instances. Therefore there is no risk that a printOn: message is sent to one of its instance and cause an error because no method operatorString is found.

The code would have looked like the following:

```
EAddition >> operatorString
    ^ ' + '
```

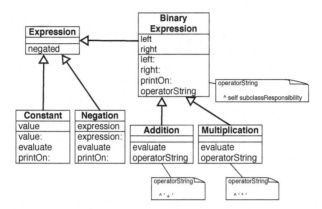

Figure 16-10 Better design: Declaring an abstract method as a way to document a hook method.

```
EMultiplication >> operatorString
  ^ ' * '
```

Now such a design is not really good because as potential extenders, developers will have to guess reading the subclass definitions that they should also define a method operatorString. A better solution in that case is to define an *abstract* method in the superclass as follows:

```
EBinaryExpression >> operatorString
  ^ self subclassResponsibility
```

Using the message subclassResponsibility declares that a method is abstract and does nothing except forcing its redefinition: subclasses should redefine it explicitly. Using such an approach we get the final situation represented in Figure 16-10.

In the solution presented before (section 16.13) we decided to go for the simplest solution and it was to use one of the default value (' + ') as a default definition for the hook in the superclass EExpression. It was not a good solution and we did it on purpose to be able to have this discussion. It was not a good solution since it was using a specific subclass. It is better to define a default value for a hook in the superclass when this default value makes sense in the class itself.

Note that we could also define evaluate as an abstract method in EExpression to indicate clearly that each subclass should define an evaluate.

16.16 Variables

Up until now our mathematical expressions are rather limited. We only manipulate constant-based expressions. What we would like is to be able to manipulate variables too. Here is a simple test to show what we mean: we define a variable named 'x' and then we can later specify that 'x' should take a given value.

Let us create a new test class named EVariableTest and define a first test testValueOfx.

```
EVariableTest >> testValueOfx
  self assert: ((EVariable new id: #x) evaluateWith: {#x -> 10}
    asDictionary) equals: 10.
```

Some technical points

Let us explain a bit what we are doing with the expression {#x -> 10} asDictionary. We should be able to specify that a given variable name is associated with a given value. For this we create a dictionary: a dictionary is a data structure for storing keys and their associated value. Here a key is the variable and the value its associated value. Let us present some details first.

Dictionaries

A dictionary is a data structure containing pairs (key value) and we can access the value of a given key. It can use any object as key and any object as values. Here we simply use a symbol #x since symbols are unique within the system and as such we are sure that we cannot have two keys looking the same but having different values.

```
| d |
d := Dictionary new
  at: #x put: 33;
  at: #y put: 52;
  at: #z put: 98.
d at: y
>>> 52
```

The previous dictionary can be easily expressed more compactly using {#x -> 33 . #y -> 52 . #z -> 98} asDictionary.

```
{#x -> 33 . #y -> 52 . #z -> 98} asDictionary at: #y
>>> 52
```

Dynamic Arrays

The expression { } creates a dynamic array. Dynamic arrays execute their expressions and store the resulting values.

```
{2 + 3 . 6 - 2 . 7-2 }
>>> ==#(5 4 5)==
```

Pairs

The expression #x -> 10 creates a pair with a key and a value.

```
| p |
p := #x -> 10.
p key
>>> #x
p value
>>> 10
```

Back to variable expressions

If we go a step further, we want to be able to build more complex expressions where instead of having constants we can manipulate variables. This way we will be able to build more advanced behavior such as expression derivations.

```
EExpression subclass: #EVariable
   instanceVariableNames: 'id'
   classVariableNames: ''
   package: 'Expressions'
```

```
EVariable >> id: aSymbol
   id := aSymbol
```

```
EVariable >> printOn: aStream
   aStream nexPutAll: id asString
```

What we see is that we need to be able to pass bindings (a binding is a pair key, value) when evaluating a variable. The value of a variable is the value of the binding whose key is the name of the variable.

```
EVariable >> evaluateWith: aBindingDictionary
   ^ aBindingDictionary at: id
```

Your tests should all pass at this point.

For more complex expressions (the ones that interest us) here are two tests.

```
EVariableTest >> testValueOfxInNegation
   self assert: ((EVariable new id: #x) negated
     evaluateWith: {#x -> 10} asDictionary) equals: -10
```

What the second test shows is that we can have an expression and given a different set of bindings the value of the expression will differ.

```
EVariableTest >> testEvaluateXplusY
   | ep1 ep2 add |
   ep1 := EVariable new id: #x.
   ep2 := EVariable new id: #y.
   add := EAddition left: ep1 right: ep2.

   self assert: (add evaluateWith: { #x -> 10 . #y -> 2 }
```

```
    asDictionary) equals: 12.
  self assert: (add evaluateWith: { #x -> 10 . #y -> 12 }
    asDictionary) equals: 22
```

Non working approaches

A non working solution would be to add the following method to EExpression

```
EEXpression >> evaluateWith: aDictionary
  ^ self evaluate
```

However it does not work for at least the following reasons:

- It does not use its argument. It only works for trees composed out exclusively of constant.

- When we send a message evaluateWith: to an addition, this message is then turned into an evaluate message sent to its subexpression and such subexpression do not get an evaluateWith: message but an evaluate.

Alternatively we could add the binding to the variable itself and only provide an evaluate message as follows:

```
(EVariable new id: #x) bindings: { #x -> 10 . #y -> 2 } asDictionary
```

But it fully defeats the purpose of what a variable is. We should be able to give different values to a variable embedded inside a complex expression.

The solution: adding evaluateWith:

We should transform all the implementations and message sends from evaluate to evaluateWith: Since this is a tedious task we will use the method refactoring *Add Parameter*. Since a refactoring applies itself on the complete system, we should be a bit cautious because other Pharo classes implement methods named evaluate and we do not want to impact them.

So here are the steps that we should follow.

- Select the Expression package

- Choose Browse Scoped (it brings a browser with only your package)

- Using this browser, select a method evaluate

- Select the *Add Parameter* refactoring: type evaluateWith: as method selector and proceed when prompted for a default value Dictionary new. This last expression is needed because the engine will rewrite all the messages evaluate but evaluateWith: Dictionary new.

- The system is performing many changes. Check that they only touch your classes and accept them all.

A test like the following one:

```
EConstant >> testEvaluate
  self assert: (EConstant constant5) evaluate equals: 5
```

is transformed as follows:

```
EConstant >> testEvaluate
  self assert: ((EConstant constant5) evaluateWith: Dictionary new)
    equals: 5
```

Your tests should nearly all pass except the ones on variables. Why do they fail? Because the refactoring transformed message sends evaluate but evaluateWith: Dictionary new and this even in methods evaluate.

```
EAddition >> evaluateWith: anObject
  ^ (right evaluateWith: Dictionary new) + (left evaluateWith:
    Dictionary new)
```

This method should be transformed as follows: We should pass the binding to the argument of the evaluateWith: recursive calls.

```
EAddition >> evaluateWith: anObject
  ^ (right evaluateWith: anObject) + (left evaluateWith: anObject)
```

Do the same for the multiplications.

```
ENegation >> evaluateWith: anObject
  ^ (expression evaluateWith: anObject) negated
```

16.17 Conclusion

This little exercise was full of learning potential. Here is a little summary of what we explained and we hope you understood.

- A message specifies an intent while a method is a named list of execution. We often have one message and a list of methods with the same name.

- Sending a message is finding the method corresponding to the message selector: this selection is based on the class of the object receiving the message. When we look for a method we start in the class of the receiver and go up the inheritance link.

- Tests are a really nice way to specify what we want to achieve and then to verify after each change that we did not break something. Tests do not prevent bugs but they help us building confidence in the changes we do by identifying fast errors.

- Refactorings are more than simple code transformations. Usually refactorings pay attention that their application does not change the behavior of program. As we saw refactorings are powerful operations that really help doing complex operations in a few actions.

- We saw that the introduction of a new superclass and moving instance variables or method to a superclass does not change the structure or behavior of the subclasses. This is because (1) for the state, the structure of an instance is based on the state of its class and all its superclasses, (2) the lookup starts in the class of the receiver and look in superclasses.

- Each time we send a message, we create a potential place (a hook) for subclasses to get their code definition used in place of the superclass's one.

Part V

Little projects

17

A simple network simulator

In this chapter, we develop a simulator for a computer network, step by step from scratch. The program starts with a simplistic model of a computer network, made of objects that represent different parts of a local network such as packets, nodes, workstations, routers and hubs.

At first, we will just simulate the different steps of packet delivery and have fun with the system. In a second step we will extend the basic functionalities by adding extensions such as a hub and different packet routing strategies. Doing so, we will revisit many object-oriented concepts such as polymorphism, encapsulation, hooks and templates. Finally this system could be refined to become an experiment platform to explore and understand distributed algorithms.

Basic definitions and a starting point

We need to establish the basic model; what does the description above tell us? A network is a number of interconnected nodes, which exchange data packets. We will therefore probably need to model the nodes, the connection links, and the packets:

- Nodes have addresses, can send and receive packets;

- Links connect two nodes together, and transmit packets between them;

- A packet transports a payload and has the address of the node to which it should be delivered; if we want nodes to be able to answer (after reception), packets should also have the address of the node which originally sent it.

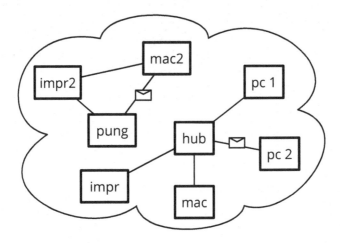

Figure 17-1 Two little networks composed of nodes and sending packets over links.

17.1 Packets are simple value objects

Packets seem to be the simplest objects in our model: we need to create them, and ask them about the data they contain, and that's about it. Once created, a packet object is merely a passive data structure: it will not change its data, knows nothing of the surrounding network, and has no behavior that we can really talk about.

Let's start by defining a test class and a first test sketching what creating and looking at packets would look like:

```
TestCase subclass: #KANetworkEntitiesTest
    instanceVariableNames: ''
    classVariableNames: ''
    category: 'NetworkSimulator-Tests'
```

```
KANetworkEntitiesTest >> testPacketCreation
    | src dest payload packet |
    src := Object new.
    dest := Object new.
    payload := Object new.

    packet := KANetworkPacket from: src to: dest payload: payload.

    self assert: packet sourceAddress equals: src.
    self assert: packet destinationAddress equals: dest.
    self assert: packet payload equals: payload
```

By writing this unit test, we described how we think packets should be created, using a from:to:payload: constructor message, and how it should be accessed, using three messages `sourceAddress`, `destinationAddress`, and `payload`. Since we have not yet decided what addresses and payloads should look like, we just pass arbitrary objects as parameters; all that matters is that when we ask the packet, it returns the correct object back.

Of course, if we now compile and run this test method, it will fail, because the class `KANetworkPacket` has not been created yet, nor any of the four above messages. You can either execute and let the system prompt you when needed or we can define the class:

```
Object subclass: #KANetworkPacket
    instanceVariableNames: 'sourceAddress destinationAddress payload'
    classVariableNames: ''
    category: 'NetworkSimulator-Core'
```

The class-side constructor method creates an instance, which it returns after sending it an initialization message; nothing original as far as constructors go:

```
KANetworkPacket class >> from: sourceAddress to: destinationAddress
    payload: anObject
    ... Your code ...
```

That constructor will need to pass the initialization parameters to the new instance. It's preferable to define a single initialization method that takes all needed parameters at once, since it is only supposed to be called when creating packets and should not be confused with a setter:

```
KANetworkPacket >> initializeSource: source destination: destination
    payload: anObject
    ... Your code ...
```

Once a packet is created, all we need to do with it is to obtain its payload, or the addresses of its source or destination nodes. Define the following getters:

```
KANetworkPacket >> sourceAddress
    ... Your code ...
KANetworkPacket >> destinationAddress
    ... Your code ...
KANetworkPacket >> payload
    ... Your code ...
```

Now our test should be running and passing. That's enough for our admittedly simplistic model of packets; we completely ignore the layers of the OSI model, but it could be an interesting exercise to model them more precisely.

17.2 Nodes are known by their address

The first obvious thing we can say about a network node is that if we want to be able to send packets to it, then it should have an address; let's translate that into a test:

```
KANetworkEntitiesTest >> testNodeCreation
    | address node |
    address := Object new.
    node := KANetworkNode withAddress: address.
    self assert: node address equals: address
```

Like before, to run this test to completion, we will have to define the KANetworkNode class:

```
Object subclass: #KANetworkNode
    instanceVariableNames: 'address'
    classVariableNames: ''
    category: 'NetworkSimulator-Core'
```

Then a class-side constructor method taking the address of the new node as parameter:

```
KANetworkNode class >> withAddress: aNetworkAddress
    ^ self new
        initializeAddress: aNetworkAddress;
        yourself
```

The constructor relies on an instance-side initialization method, and the test asserts that the address accessor works; define them:

```
KANetworkNode >> initializeAddress: aNetworkAddress
    ... Your code ...
KANetworkNode >> address
    ... Your code ...
```

Again, our simplistic tests should now pass.

17.3 Links are one-way connections between nodes

After nodes and packets, what about looking at links? In the real world, network cables are bidirectional, but that's because they have wires going both ways. Here, we're going to keep it simple and define links as simple one-way connections; to make a two-way connection, we will just use two links, one in each direction.

However, creating links that know their source and destination nodes is not sufficient: *nodes* also need to know about their outgoing links, otherwise they cannot send packets. Let us write a test to cover this.

```
KANetworkEntitiesTest >> testNodeLinking
    | node1 node2 link |
    node1 := KANetworkNode withAddress: #address1.
    node2 := KANetworkNode withAddress: #address2.
    link := KANetworkLink from: node1 to: node2.
```

```
    link attach.

    self assert: (node1 hasLinkTo: node2)
```

This test creates two nodes and a link; after telling the link to *attach* itself, we check that it did so: the source node should confirm that it has an outgoing link to the destination node. Note that the constructor could have registered the link with node1, but we opted for a separate message attach instead, because it's bad form to have a constructor change other objets; this way we can build links between arbitrary nodes and still have control of when the connection really becomes part of the network model. For symmetry, we could have specified that node2 has an incoming link from node1, but that ends up not being necessary, so we leave that out for now.

Again, we need to define the class of links:

```
Object subclass: #KANetworkLink
    instanceVariableNames: 'source destination'
    classVariableNames: ''
    category: 'NetworkSimulator-Core'
```

A constructor that passes the two required parameters to an instance-side initialization message:

```
KANetworkLink class >> from: sourceNode to: destinationNode
    ^ self new
        initializeFrom: sourceNode to: destinationNode
```

As well as the initialization method and accessors:

```
KANetworkLink >> initializeFrom: sourceNode to: destinationNode
    ... Your code ...
KANetworkLink >> source
    ... Your code ...
KANetworkLink >> destination
    ... Your code ...
```

The attach method of a link should not (and cannot) directly modify the source node, so it must delegate to it instead.

```
KANetworkLink >> attach
    source attach: self
```

This is an example of separation of concerns: the link knows which node has to do what, but only the node itself knows precisely how to do that. Here, if a node knows about all its outgoing links, it means it has a collection of those, and attaching a link adds it to that collection:

```
KANetworkNode >> attach: anOutgoingLink
    outgoingLinks add: anOutgoingLink
```

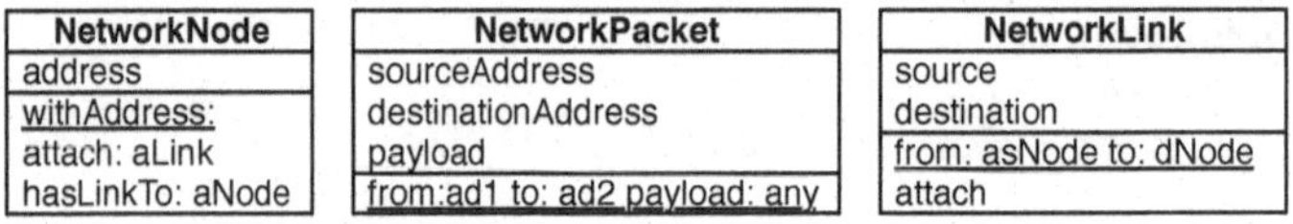

NetworkNode	NetworkPacket	NetworkLink
address	sourceAddress	source
withAddress:	destinationAddress	destination
attach: aLink	payload	from: asNode to: dNode
hasLinkTo: aNode	from:ad1 to: ad2 payload: any	attach

Figure 17-2   Current API of our three main classes.

For this method to compile correctly, we will need to extend KANetworkNode with the new instance variable outgoingLinks, and with the corresponding initialization code:

```
KANetworkNode >> initialize
    outgoingLinks := Set new.
```

And finally the unit test relied on a predicate method to define in KANetworkNode:

```
KANetworkNode >> hasLinkTo: anotherNode
    ... Your code ...
```

The method hasLinkTo: should verify that there is at least one outgoing links whose destination is the node passed as argument. We suggest to have a look at the iterator anySatisfy: to express this logic.

Again, all the tests should now pass.

17.4   Making our objects more understandable

When programming we often make mistakes and it is important to help developer to address them. Le us put a breakpoint and try to understand the objects.

```
KANetworkEntitiesTest >> testNodeLinking
    | node1 node2 link |
    node1 := KANetworkNode withAddress: #address1.
    node2 := KANetworkNode withAddress: #address2.
    link := KANetworkLink from: node1 to: node2.
    link attach.
    self halt.
    self assert: (node1 hasLinkTo: node2)
```

Running the test will open a debugger as the one shown in Figure 17-3. We get object but their textual representation is too generic to really help us.

The method printOn: is responsible to the printing of the object representation. We will then redefine this method for the different objects we have.

```
KANetworkNode >> printOn: aStream
    aStream nextPutAll: 'Node ('.
    aStream nextPutAll: address , ')'
```

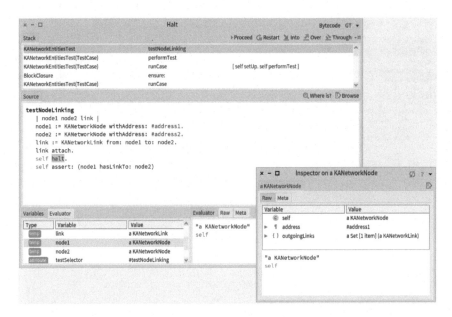

Figure 17-3 Navigating specific objects having a generic presentation.

```
KANetworkLink >> printOn: aStream
    aStream nextPutAll: 'Link'.
    source
        ifNotNil: [ aStream
                nextPutAll: ' ';
                nextPutAll: source address ].
    destination
        ifNotNil: [ aStream
                nextPutAll: ' -> ';
                nextPutAll: destination address ]
```

Now if we rerun the test we obtain a better user experience as shown in Figure 17-4: we can see the address of a node and the source and destination of a link.

17.5 Simulating the steps of packet delivery

The next big feature is that nodes should be able to send and receive packets, and links to transmit them.

```
KANetworkEntitiesTest >> testSendAndTransmit
    | srcNode destNode link packet |
    srcNode := KANetworkNode withAddress: #src.
    destNode := KANetworkNode withAddress: #dest.
```

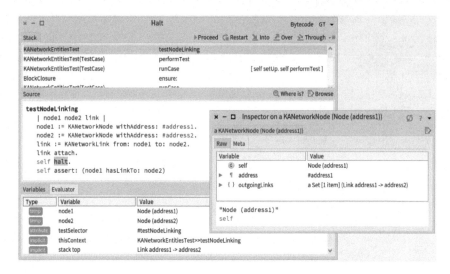

Figure 17-4 Navigating objects offering a customized presentation.

```
link := (KANetworkLink from: srcNode to: destNode) attach;
yourself.
packet := KANetworkPacket from: #address to: #dest payload:
#payload.

srcNode send: packet via: link.
self assert: (link isTransmitting: packet).
self deny: (destNode hasReceived: packet).

link transmit: packet.
self deny: (link isTransmitting: packet).
self assert: (destNode hasReceived: packet)
```

We create and setup two nodes, a link between them, and a packet. Now, to control which packets get delivered in which order, we specify that it happens in separate, controlled steps. This will allow us to model packet delivery precisely, to simulate latency, out-of-order reception, etc.:

- First, we tell the node to send the packet using the message send:via:. At that point, the packet should be passed to the link for transmission, but not completely delivered yet.

- Then, we tell the link to actually transmit the packet along using the message transmit:, and thus the packet should be received by the destination node.

17.6 **Sending a packet**

To send a packet, the node emits it on the link:

```
KANetworkNode >> send: aPacket via: aLink
    aLink emit: aPacket
```

For the simulation to be realistic, we do not want the packet to be delivered right away; instead, emitting a packet really just stores it in the link, until the user elects this packet to proceed using the transmit: message. Storing packets requires adding an instance variable to KANetworkLink, as well as specifying how this instance variable should be initialized.

```
Object subclass: #KANetworkLink
    instanceVariableNames: 'source destination packetsToTransmit'
    classVariableNames: ''
    category: 'NetworkSimulator-Core'
```

```
KANetworkLink >> initialize
    packetsToTransmit := OrderedCollection new
```

```
KANetworkLink >> emit: aPacket
    "Packets are not transmitted right away, but stored.
    Transmission is explicitly triggered later, by sending
    #transmit:."

    packetsToTransmit add: aPacket
```

We also add a testing method to check whether a given packet is currently being transmitted by a link:

```
KANetworkLink >> isTransmitting: aPacket
    ... Your code ...
```

17.7 **Transmitting across a link**

Transmitting a packet means telling the link's destination node to receive it. Nodes only consume packets addressed to them; fortunately this is what will happen in our test, so we can worry about the alternative case later (notYetImplemented is a special message that we can use in place of code that we will have to write eventually, but prefer to ignore for now).

```
KANetworkNode >> receive: aPacket from: aLink
    aPacket destinationAddress = address
        ifTrue: [
            self consume: aPacket.
            arrivedPackets add: aPacket ]
        ifFalse: [ self notYetImplemented ]
```

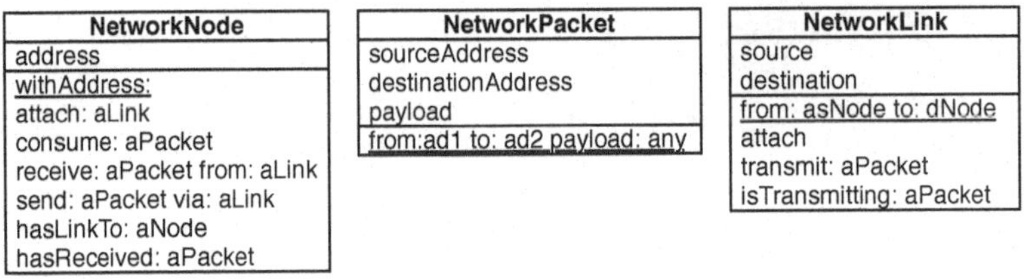

NetworkNode	NetworkPacket	NetworkLink
address	sourceAddress	source
withAddress:	destinationAddress	destination
attach: aLink	payload	from: asNode to: dNode
consume: aPacket	from:ad1 to: ad2 payload: any	attach
receive: aPacket from: aLink		transmit: aPacket
send: aPacket via: aLink		isTransmitting: aPacket
hasLinkTo: aNode		
hasReceived: aPacket		

Figure 17-5   Richer API.

Consuming a packet represents what the node will do with it at the application level; for now let's just define an empty consume: method, as a placeholder:

```
KANetworkNode >> consume: aPacket
    "Default handling is to do nothing."
```

After consuming the packet, we remember it did arrive; this is mostly for testing and debugging, but someday we might want to simulate packet losses and re-emissions. Don't forget to declare and initialize the arrivedPackets instance variable, along with its accessor:

```
KANetworkNode >> hasReceived: aPacket
    ... Your code ...
```

Now we can implement the transmit: message. A link can not transmit packets that have not been sent via it, and once transmitted, the packet should not be on the link anymore. We should remove it from the link list of package to be transmitted and tell the destination to receive it using the message receive:from:.

```
KANetworkLink >> transmit: aPacket
    "Transmit aPacket to the destination node of the receiver link."
    ... Your code ...
```

At that point all our tests should pass. Note that the message notYetImplemented is not called, since our tests do not yet require routing. Figure 17-5 shows that the API of our classes is getting richer than before.

17.8   The loopback link

On a real network, when a node wants to send a packet to itself, it does not need any connection to do so. In real-world networking stacks, loopback routing shortcuts the lower networking layers; however, this is finer detail than we are modeling here.

Still, we want to model the fact that the loopback link is a little special, so each node will store its own loopback link, separately from the outgoing links. We start to define a test.

```
KANetworkEntitiesTest >> testLoopback
    | node packet |
    node := KANetworkNode withAddress: #address.
    packet := KANetworkPacket from: #address to: #address payload:
    #payload.

    node send: packet.
    node loopback transmit: packet.

    self assert: (node hasReceived: packet).
    self deny: (node loopback isTransmitting: packet)
```

The loopback link is implicitly created as part of the node itself. We also introduce a new send: message, which takes the responsibility of selecting the link to emit the packet. For triggering packet transmission, we have to use a specific accessor to find the loopback link of the node.

First, we have to add yet another instance variable in nodes:

```
Object subclass: #KANetworkNode
    instanceVariableNames: 'address outgoingLinks loopback
    arrivedPackets'
    classVariableNames: ''
    category: 'NetworkSimulator-Core'
```

As with all instance variables, we have to remember to make sure it is correctly initialized; we thus modify initialize:

```
KANetworkNode >> initialize
    ... Your code ...
```

The accessor has nothing special:

```
KANetworkNode >> loopback
    ^ loopback
```

And finally we can focus on the send: method and automatic link selection. The method send: should be more generic than the method send:via: and will be one exposed as a public entry point.

This method has to rely on some routing algorithm to identify which links will transmit the packet closer to its destination. Since some routing algorithms select more than one link, we will implement routing as an *iteration* method, which evaluates the given block for each selected link.

```
KANetworkNode >> send: aPacket
    "Send aPacket, leaving the responsibility of routing to the
    node."
    self
        linksTowards: aPacket destinationAddress
        do: [ :link | self send: aPacket via: link ]
```

One of the simplest routing algorithm is *flooding*: just send the packet via every outgoing link. Obviously, this is a waste of bandwidth, but it works without any knowledge of the network topology beyond the list of outgoing links.

However, there is one case where we know how to route the packet: if the destination address matches the one of the current node, we can select the loopback link alone. The logic of linksTowards:do: is then to check is the address we want to send the packet is the one of the node. In that case we execute the block using the loopback link, else we simple iterate on the outgoing links of the receiver.

```
KANetworkNode >> linksTowards: anAddress do: aBlock
    "Simple flood algorithm: route via all outgoing links.
    However, just loopback if the receiver node is the routing
    destination."
    ... Your code ...
```

Now we have the basic model working, and we can try more realistic examples.

17.9 Modeling the network itself

More realistic tests will require non-trivial networks. We thus need an object that represents the network as a whole, to avoid keeping many nodes and links in individual variables. We will introduce a new class KANetwork, whose responsibility is to help us build, assemble then find the nodes and links involved in a network.

Let's start by creating another test class, to keep things in order:

```
TestCase subclass: #KANetworkTest
    instanceVariableNames: 'net hub alone'
    classVariableNames: ''
    category: 'NetworkSimulator-Tests'
```

Since every test needs to rebuild the whole example network from scratch, we specify so in the setUp method:

```
KANetworkTest >> setUp
    self buildNetwork
```

Before anything else, let's write a test that will pass once we've made progress; we want to access network nodes given only their addresses. Here we check that we get a hub node based on its address:

```
KANetworkTest >> testNetworkFindsNodesByAddress
    self
        assert: (net nodeAt: hub address ifNone: [ self fail ])
        equals: hub
```

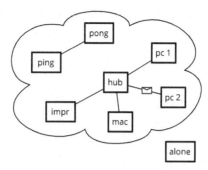

Figure 17-6   A hub.

We will have to implement this nodeAt:ifNone: on our KANetwork class; but first we need to decide how its instances are built. Let's build network net, with the main part connected in a star shape around a hub node; a pair of nodes ping and pong are part of the network but not connected to hub, and the alone node is just by itself, not even added to the network as shown in Figure 17-6.

Expanding a network implies adding new connections and possibly new nodes to it. If the net object understands a connect: aNode to: anotherNode message, you should be able to build nodes and connect them into a network that matches the figure.

```
KANetworkTest >> buildNetwork
    alone := KANetworkNode withAddress: #alone.
    net := KANetwork new.
    hub := KANetworkNode withAddress: #hub.
    #(mac pc1 pc2 prn)
        do: [ :addr |
            | node |
            node := KANetworkNode withAddress: addr.
            net connect: node to: hub ].
    net connect: (KANetworkNode withAddress: #ping) to:
    (KANetworkNode withAddress: #pong)
```

The name of the connect:to: message suggests that establishing the bidirectional links is the responsibility of the net object. It also has to remember enough info so we can inspect the network topology; we can simply store nodes and links in a couple of sets, even though that representation is a little redundant. Let's define the class with two instance variables:

```
Object subclass: #KANetwork
    instanceVariableNames: 'nodes links'
    classVariableNames: ''
    category: 'NetworkSimulator-Core'
```

Whenever we define an instance variable, initialization comes next:

```
KANetwork >> initialize
    ... Your code ...
```

Now we can give the network the possibility to create links. This method we will use to add links to the network link collection.

```
KANetwork >> makeLinkFrom: aNode to: anotherNode
  ^ KANetworkLink from: aNode to: anotherNode
```

We add a low level method add: to add a node in a network.

```
KANetwork >> add: aNode
    nodes add: aNode
```

To be able to test the network construction we add a little test message;

```
KANetwork >> doesRecordNode: aNode
    ^ nodes includes: aNode
```

Now, we can add isolated nodes to the network, even if it does not seem very useful.

Connecting nodes.

Connecting nodes without ensuring that they are part of the network really does not make sense. Therefore, when connecting nodes, we will first ensure the nodes are added (by simply adding them in the node Set of the network), then we create and attach links in *both* directions; finally we store both links.

Here is a test covering this aspect.

```
KANetworkTest >> testConnect
  | netw hubb mac pc1 |
  netw := KANetwork new.
  hubb := KANetworkNode withAddress: #hub.
  mac := KANetworkNode withAddress: #mac.
  pc1 := KANetworkNode withAddress: #pc1.

  netw connect: hubb to: mac.
  self assert: (hubb hasLinkTo: mac).
  self assert: (mac hasLinkTo: hubb).
  self assert: (netw doesRecordNode: hubb).
  self assert: (netw doesRecordNode: mac).

  netw connect: hubb to: pc1.
  self assert: (hubb hasLinkTo: pc1).
  self assert: (mac hasLinkTo: hubb)
```

Now implement the connect:to: method; for concision, note that the attach method we defined previously effectively returns the link.

```
KANetwork >> connect: aNode to: anotherNode
    ... Your code ...
```

The test testConnect should be green.

17.10   Looking up nodes

At this point, the test testNetworkFindsNodesByAddress should run through setUp but fail in the unit test itself, because we still need to implement node lookup. The base lookup should find the first node that has the requested address, or evaluate a fall-back block (a perfect case for the detect:ifNone: message):

```
KANetwork >> nodeAt: anAddress ifNone: noneBlock
    ... Your code ...
```

We can also make a convenience nodeAt: method for node lookup, that will raise the predefined NotFound exception if it does not find the node. Let's first write a test which validates this behavior:

```
KANetworkTest >> testNetworkOnlyFindsAddedNodes
    self
        should: [ net nodeAt: alone address ]
        raise: NotFound
```

Then we can simply express nodeAt: by delegating to nodeAt:ifNone:. Note that raise an exception, you simply send the message signal to the exception class. Here we use the specific class method signalFor:in: defined on the NotFound class.

```
KANetwork >> nodeAt: anAddress
    ^ self
        nodeAt: anAddress
        ifNone: [ NotFound signalFor: anAddress in: self ]
```

17.11   Looking up links

Next, we want to be able to lookup links between two nodes. Again we define a new test:

```
KANetworkTest >> testNetworkFindsLinks
    | link |
    self
        shouldnt: [ link := net linkFrom: #pong to: #ping ]
        raise: NotFound.
    self
        assert: link source
        equals: (net nodeAt: #pong).
    self
        assert: link destination
```

```
    equals: (net nodeAt: #ping)
```

And we define the method `linkFrom:to:` returning the link between source
and destination nodes with matching addresses, and signalling `NotFound` if
no such link is found:

```
KANetwork >> linkFrom: sourceAddress to: destinationAddress
    ... Your code ...
```

Final check.

As a final check, let's try some of the previous tests, first on the isolated
`alone` node, showing that loopback works even without a network connection:

```
KANetworkTest >> testSelfSend
    | packet |
    packet := KANetworkPacket
        from: alone address
        to: alone address
        payload: #something.
    self assert: (packet isAddressedTo: alone).
    self assert: (packet isOriginatingFrom: alone).

    alone send: packet.
    self deny: (alone hasReceived: packet).
    self assert: (alone loopback isTransmitting: packet).

    alone loopback transmit: packet.
    self deny: (alone loopback isTransmitting: packet).
    self assert: (alone hasReceived: packet)
```

You can see that we used new convenience testing methods `isAddressedTo:`
and `isOriginatingFrom:` which help inspect the state of a simulated network without explicitly comparing addresses. However, those methods should
not take part in network simulation code, since in the real world nodes can
never know their peers other than through their addresses.

```
KANetworkPacket >> isAddressedTo: aNode
    ^ destinationAddress = aNode address
```

```
KANetworkPacket >> isOriginatingFrom: aNode
    ^ sourceAddress = aNode address
```

The second test attempts transmitting a packet in the network, between the
directly connected nodes `ping` and `pong`:

```
KANetworkTest >> testDirectSend
    | packet ping pong link |
    packet := KANetworkPacket from: #ping to: #pong payload: #ball.
    ping := net nodeAt: #ping.
    pong := net nodeAt: #pong.
```

```
link := net linkFrom: #ping to: #pong.

ping send: packet.
self assert: (link isTransmitting: packet).
self deny: (pong hasReceived: packet).

link transmit: packet.
self deny: (link isTransmitting: packet).
self assert: (pong hasReceived: packet)
```

Both tests should pass with no additional work, since they just reproduce what we already tested in `KANetworkEntitiesTest` and adding `KANetwork` did not impact the established behavior of nodes, links, and packets.

17.12   Packet delivery with forwarding

Until now, we only tested packet delivery between directly connected nodes; let's try sending a node so that the packet has to be forwarded through the hub.

```
KANetworkTest >> testSendViaHub
    | hello mac pc1 firstLink secondLink |
    hello := KANetworkPacket from: #mac to: #pc1 payload: 'Hello!'.
    mac := net nodeAt: #mac.
    pc1 := net nodeAt: #pc1.
    firstLink := net linkFrom: #mac to: #hub.
    secondLink := net linkFrom: #hub to: #pc1.

    self assert: (hello isAddressedTo: pc1).
    self assert: (hello isOriginatingFrom: mac).

    mac send: hello.
    self deny: (pc1 hasReceived: hello).
    self assert: (firstLink isTransmitting: hello).

    firstLink transmit: hello.
    self deny: (pc1 hasReceived: hello).
    self assert: (secondLink isTransmitting: hello).

    secondLink transmit: hello.
    self assert: (pc1 hasReceived: hello).
```

If you run this test, you will see that it fails because of the `notYetImple-mented` message we left earlier in `receive:from:`; it's time to fix that! When a node receives a packet but is not the recipient, it should forward the packet:

```
KANetworkNode >> receive: aPacket from: aLink
    aPacket destinationAddress = address
        ifTrue: [
            self consume: aPacket.
            arrivedPackets add: aPacket ]
        ifFalse: [ self forward: aPacket from: aLink ]
```

Now we need to implement packet forwarding, but there is a trap. An easy solution would be to simply send: the packet again: the hub would send the packet to all its connected nodes, one of which happens to be pc1, the recipient, so all is good!

Wrong...

The packet would be also sent to other nodes than the recipient; what would those nodes do when they receive a packet not addressed to them? Forward it. Where? To all their neighbours, which would forward it again... so when would the forwarding stop?

To fix this, we need hubs to behave differently from nodes. In reality, hubs work at the lower layers of the OSI model, but our simplified model does not have that level of detail. We can approximate this by saying that upon reception of a packet addressed to another node, a hub should forward the packet, but a normal node should just ignore it.

Let's first define an empty forward:from: method for nodes, then add a new class for hubs, which will be modeled as nodes with an actual implementation of forwarding:

```
KANetworkNode >> forward: aPacket from: arrivalLink
    "Do nothing. Normal nodes do not route packets."
```

17.13 Introducing a new kind of node

Now we define the class KANetworkHub that will be the recipient of hub specific behavior.

```
KANetworkNode subclass: #KANetworkHub
    instanceVariableNames: ''
    classVariableNames: ''
    category: 'NetworkSimulator'
```

A hub does not have routing information, so all it can do is flood routing, with a catch: the packet must not be sent back from where it arrived, because if that happens to be another hub the packet would bounce back and forth indefinitely. We suggest to take advantage of the message linksTowards:do: that performs an action for all given links to one address.

```
KANetworkHub >> forward: aPacket from: arrivalLink
    ... Your code ...
```

Now we can use a proper hub in our test, replacing the relevant line in `KANet`-`workTest >> buildNetwork`, and check that the `testSendViaHub` unit test passes.

```
[   hub := KANetworkHub withAddress: #hub.
```

You have now a nice basis for network simulation. In the following we will present some possible extensions.

17.14   Other examples of specialized nodes

In this section we will present some extensions of the core to support different scenarios. We will propose some tasks to make sure that the extensions are fully working. In addition in this section we do not define tests and we strongly encourage you to start to write tests. At the moment of the book you should be ready to write your own tests and see their values to improve your development process. So take this opportunity to practice.

Workstations counting received packets

We would like to know how many packets specific nodes are receiving. In particular when a workstation consumes a packet, it simply increments a packet counter.

Let's start by subclassing `KANetworkNode`:

```
KANetworkNode subclass: #KANetworkWorkstation
    instanceVariableNames: 'receivedCount'
    classVariableNames: ''
    category: 'NetworkSimulator-Nodes'
```

We need to initialize the `receivedCount` instance variable. Properly redefining `initialize` is enough, because the address is initialized separately in the constructor method `KANetworkNode >> withAddress:`; however, it's really important not to forget the `super initialize` message, because that method does initialize the default node behavior.

```
KANetworkWorkstation >> initialize
    super initialize.
    receivedCount := 0
```

Now we can redefine `consume:` accordingly:

```
KANetworkWorkstation >> consume: aPacket
    receivedCount := receivedCount + 1
```

Define accessors and the `printOn:` method for debugging. Define a test for the behavior of workstation nodes.

Printers accumulating printouts

When a printer consumes a packet, it prints it; we can model the output tray as a list where packet payloads get queued, and the supply tray as the number of blank sheets it contains.

The implementation is very similar; we subclass KANetworkNode to redefine the consume: method:

```
KANetworkNode subclass: #KANetworkPrinter
    instanceVariableNames: 'supply tray'
    classVariableNames: ''
    category: 'NetworkSimulator-Nodes'
```

```
KANetworkPrinter >> consume: aPacket
    supply > 0 ifTrue: [ ^ self "no paper, do nothing" ].

    supply := supply - 1.
    tray add: aPacket payload
```

Initialization is a bit different, though; since the standard initialize method has no argument, the only sensible initial value for the supply instance variable is zero:

```
KANetworkPrinter >> initialize
    super initialize.
    supply := 0.
    tray := OrderedCollection new
```

We therefore need a way to pass the initial supply of paper available to a fresh instance:

```
KANetworkPrinter >> resupply: paperSheets
    supply := supply + paperSheets
```

For convenience, we can provide an extended constructor to create printers with a non-empty supply in one message:

```
KANetworkPrinter class >> withAddress: anAddress initialSupply:
    paperSheets
    ^ (self withAddress: anAddress)
        resupply: paperSheets;
        yourself
```

Define accessors and the printOn: method for debugging purpose. Define some test method for the behavior of printer nodes.

Servers answering requests

When a server node consumes a packet, it converts the payload to uppercase, then sends that back to the sender of the request.

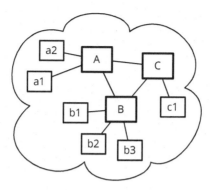

Figure 17-7   A possible extension: a more realistic network with a cycle between three router nodes.

This is yet another subclass which redefines the consume: method, but this time the node is stateless, so we have no initialization or accessor methods to write:

```
KANetworkNode subclass: #KANetworkServer
    instanceVariableNames: ''
    classVariableNames: ''
    category: 'NetworkSimulator-Nodes'
```

```
KANetworkServer >> consume: aPacket
    | response |
    response := aPacket payload asUppercase.
    self send: (KANetworkPacket
        from: self address
        to: aPacket sourceAddress
        payload: response)
```

Define a test for the behavior of server nodes.

17.15   Conclusion

In this chapter, we built a little network simulation system, step by step. We showed the benefit of good protocol decompositions.

As a further extension, we suggest modeling a more realistic network with cycles, as shown in Figure 17-7. Making this work properly will require replacing hubs with routers and flood routing with more realistic routing algorithms.

Here is a possible setup for a new family of tests.

```
KARoutingNetworkTest >> buildNetwork
    | routers |
    net := KANetwork new.

    routers := #(A B C) collect:
        [ :each | KANetworkHub withAddress: each ].
    net connect: routers first to: routers second.
    net connect: routers second to: routers third.
    net connect: routers third to: routers first.

    #(a1 a2) do: [ :addr |
        net connect: routers first
            to: (KANetworkNode withAddress: addr) ].
    #(b1 b2 b3) do: [ :addr |
        net connect: routers second
            to: (KANetworkNode withAddress: addr) ].
    net connect: routers third
        to: (KANetworkNode withAddress: #c1)
```

CHAPTER 18

Snakes and ladders

Snakes and Ladders is a simple game suitable for teaching children how to apply rules (http://en.wikipedia.org/wiki/Snakes_and_ladders). It is dull for adults because there is absolutely no strategy involved, but this makes it easy to implement! In this chapter you will implement SnakesAndLadders and we use it as a pretext to explore design questions.

18.1 Game rules

Snakes and Ladders originated in India as part of a family of die games. The game was introduced in England as "Snakes and Ladders" (see Figure 18-1), then the basic concept was introduced in the United States as *Chutes and Ladders*. Here is a brief description of the rules:

- **Players:** Snakes and Ladders is played by two to four players, each with her/his own token to move around the board.

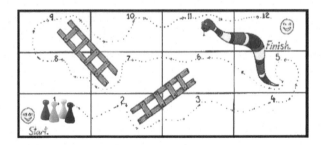

Figure 18-1 An example Snakes and Ladders board with two ladders and a snake.

- **Moving Player**: a player rolls a die, then moves the designated number of tiles, between one and six. Once he lands on a tile, she/he has to perform any action designated by the tile. (Since the rules are fuzzy we decided that we can have multiple players in the same tile).

- **Ladders:** If the tile a player lands on is at the bottom of a ladder, she/he should climb the ladder, which brings him to a tile higher on the board.

- **Snakes:** If the tile a player lands on is a head snake, she/he must slide down the snake, landing on a tile closer to the beginning.

- **Winning:** the winner is the player who gets to the last tile first, whether by landing on it from a roll, or by reaching it with a ladder. We decided that when the player does not move if he does not land directly on the last tile, it does not move.

18.2 Game possible run

The code snippet below is a possible way to program this game. We take as a board configuration the one depicted in Figure 18-1. It defines a board game composed of 12 tiles with two ladders and one snake. We add two players and then start the game.

```
| jill jack game |
game := SLGame new tileNumber: 12.
game
   setLadderFrom: 2 to: 6;
   setLadderFrom: 7 to: 9;
   setSnakeFrom: 11 to: 5.
game
   addPlayer: (SLPlayer new name: 'Jill');
   addPlayer: (SLPlayer new name: 'Jack').
game play
```

Since we want to focus on the game logic, you will develop a textual version of the game and avoid any lengthy user interface descriptions.

The following is an example game execution: Two players are on the first tile. The board contains two ladders, [2->6] and [7->9], and one snake [5<-11].

Jill rolls a die and throws a 3 and moves to the corresponding tile. Jack rolls a die and throws a 6 and moves to the corresponding tile and follow its effect, climbing the ladder at tile 7 up to tile 9. Jack and Jill continue to alternate taking turns until Jill ends up on the last tile.

```
[1<Jill><Jack>][2->6][3][4][5][6][7->9][8][9][10][5<-11][12]
<Jill>throws 3:
    [1<Jack>][2->6][3][4<Jill>][5][6][7->9][8][9][10][5<-11][12]
<Jack>throws 6:
    [1][2->6][3][4<Jill>][5][6][7->9][8][9<Jack>][10][5<-11][12]
```

```
<Jill>throws 5:
    [1][2->6][3][4][5][6][7->9][8][9<Jack><Jill>][10][5<-11][12]
<Jack>throws 1:
    [1][2->6][3][4][5][6][7->9][8][9<Jill>][10<Jack>][5<-11][12]
<Jill>throws 3:
    [1][2->6][3][4][5][6][7->9][8][9][10<Jack>][5<-11][12<Jill>]
```

18.3   **Potential objects and responsibilities**

Take a piece of paper, study the game rules and list any potential objects and their behavior. This is an important exercise to practice, training yourself to discover potential objects and classes.

Techniques such as *Responsibility Driven Design* exist to help programmers during this phase of object discovery. Responsibility Driven Design suggests analysing the documents describing a project, and turning the subjects of sentences into candidate objects and grouping verbs as the behavior of these objects. Any synonyms are identifed and used to reduce and gather together similar objects or behavior. Then later objects are grouped into classes. Some alternate approaches look for relationship patterns between objects such as part-whole, locations, entity-owner... This could be the topic of a full book.

Here we follow another path: sketching scenarios. We describe several scenarios and from such scenario we identify key playing objects.

- Scenario 1. The game is created with a number of tiles. The game must have an end and start tiles. Ladders and snakes should be declared.

- Scenario 2. Players are declared. They start on the first tiles.

- Scenario 3. When player rolls a die, he should move the number of tiles given by the die.

- Scenario 4. After moving the first player a given number of tiles based on the result of die roll, this is the turn of the second player.

- Scenario 5. When a player arrives to a ladder start, it should be moved to the ladder end.

- Scenario 6. When a player should move further than the end tile, he does not move.

- Scenario 7. When a player ends its course on the end tile, he wins and the game is finished.

Such scenarios are interesting because they are a good basis for tests.

Possible class candidates

When reading the rules and the scenario, here is a list of possible classes that we could use. We will refine it later and remove double or overlapping concepts.

- Game: keeps track of the game state, the players, and whose turn it is.
- Board: keeps the tile configuration.
- Player: keeps track of location on the board and moving over tiles.
- Tile: keeps track of any player on it.
- Snake: is a special tile which sends a player back to an earlier tile.
- Ladder: is a special tile which sends a player ahead to a later tile.
- First Tile: holds multiple players at the beginning of the game.
- Last Tile: players must land exactly on this tile, or else they do not move.
- Die: rolls and indicates the number of tiles that a player must move over.

It is not clear if all the objects we identify by looking at the problem and its scenario should be really turned into real objects. Also sometimes it is useful to get more classes to capture behavior and state variations. We should look to have an exact mapping between concepts identified in the problem scenario or description and the implementation.

From analysing this list we can draw some observations:

- Game and Board are probably the same concept and we can merge them.
- Die may be overkill. Having a full object just to produce a random number may not be worth, especially since we do not have a super fancy user interface showing the die rolling and other effect.
- Tile, Snake, Ladder, Last and First Tile all look like tiles with some variations or specific actions. We suspect that we can reuse some logic by creating an inheritance hierarchy around the concept of Tile.

About representation

We can implement the same system using different implementation choices. For example we could have only one class implementing all the game logic and it would work. Some people may also argue that this is not a bad solution.

Object-oriented design favors the distribution of the state of the system to different objects. It is often better to have objects with clear responsibilities.

Why? Because you should consider that you will have to rethink, modify or extend your system. We should be able to understand and extend easily a system to be able to reply to new requirements.

Not having a nice object-oriented decomposition for a simple game may not be a problem, as soon as you will start to model a more complex system not having a good decomposition will hurt you. Real life applications often have a lifetime up to 25 years.

In addition, imagine that we are a game designer and we want to experiment with different variations and tiles with new properties such as one super special tile changing other tiles, adding snakes before the current player to slow other participants.

18.4 About object-oriented design

When designing a system, you will often have questions that cannot be blindly and automatically answered. Often there is no definite answer. This is what is difficult with object-oriented design and this is why practicing is important.

What composes the state of an object? The state of object should characterize the object over its lifetime. For example the name of player identifies the player.

Now it may happen that some objects just because they are instances of different classes do not need the same state but still offer the same set of messages. For example the tiles and the ladder/snake tiles have probably a similar API but snake and ladder should hold information of their target tile.

We can also distinguish between the intrinsic state of an object (e.g., name of player) and the state we use to represent the collaborators of an object.

The other important and difficult question is about the relationships between the objects. For example imagine that we model a tile as an object, should this object points to the players it contains. Similarly, should a tile knows its position or just the game should know the position of each tile.

Should the game object keep the position of the players or just the player. The game should keep the players list since it should compute who is the next player.

CRC cards

Some designers use CRC (for Class Responsibility Collaborators) cards: the idea is to take the list of classes we identified above. For each of them, they write on a little card: the class name, its responsibility in one or two sentences and list its collaborators. Once this is done, they take a scenario and see how the objects can play such a scenario. Doing so they refine their design by adding more information (collaborators) to a class or merging two classes or splitting a class into multiple ones when they fill that a class has too many responsibilities.

To improve such process, some designers consider implementation concerns or alternatives and may create objects to represent such variations.

Some heuristics

To help us taking decision, that are some heuristics:

- One object should have one main responsibility.

- Move behavior close to data. If a class defines the behavior of another object, there is a good chance that other clients of this object are doing the same and create duplicated and complex logic. If an object defines a clear behavior, clients just invoke it without duplicating it.

- Prefer domain object over literal objects. As a general principle it is better to get a reference to a more general objects than a simple number. Because we can then invoke a larger set of behavior.

Kind of data passed around

Even if in Pharo, everything is an object, storing a mere integer object instead of a full tile can lead to different solutions. There is no perfect solution mainly consequences of choices and you should learn how to assess a situation to see which one has better characteristics for your problem.

Here is a question illustrating the problem: Should a ladder know the tile it forwards the player to or is the index of a tile enough?

When designing the ladder tile behavior, we should understand how we can access the target tile where the player should be moved to. If we just give the index of the target to a ladder, the tile has to be able to access the board containing the tiles else it will be impossible to access to the target tile of the ladder. The alternative, i.e., passing the tile looks nicer because it represents a natural relation and there is no need to ask the board.

Agility to adapt

In addition it is important not to get stressed, writing tests that represent parts or scenario we want to implement is a good way to make sure that we can adapt in case we discover that we missed a point.

Now this game is interesting also from a test point of view because it may be difficult to test the parts in isolation (i.e., without requiring to have a game object).

18.5 Let us get started

You will follow an iterative process and test first approach. You will take scenario implement a test and define the corresponding classes.

This game implementation raises an interesting question which is how do we test the game state without hardcoding too much implementation details in the tests themselves. Indeed tests that validate scenario only involving public messages and high-level interfaces are more likely to be stable over time and do not require modifications. Indeed if we check the exact class of certain objects you will have to change the implementation as well as the tests when modifying the implementation. In addition, since in Pharo the tests are normal clients of the objects they test, writing some tests may force us to define extra methods to access to private data.

But enough talking! Let us start by defining a test class named SLGameTest. We will see in the course of development if we define other test classes. Our feeling is that the tiles and players are objects with limited responsibility and their responsibility is best illustrated (and then tested) when they interact with each other in the context of a given game. Therefore the class SLGame-Test describes the place in which relevant scenario will occur.

Define the class SLGameTest.

```
TestCase subclass: #SLGameTest
    instanceVariableNames: ''
    classVariableNames: ''
    package: 'SnakesAndLadders'
```

One of the first scenario is that a game is composed of a certain number of tiles.

We can write a test as follows but it does not have a lot of value. At the beginning of the development, this is normal to have limited tests because we do not have enough objects to interact with.

```
SLGameTest >> testCheckingSimpleGame

    | game |
    game := SLGame new tileNumber: 12.
    self assert: game tileNumber equals: 12
```

Now we should make this test pass. Some strong advocates of TDD say that we should code the first simplest method that would make the test pass and go to the next one. Let us see what it would be (of course this method will be changed later).

First you should define the class SLGame.

```
Object subclass: #SLGame
  instanceVariableNames: 'tiles'
  classVariableNames: ''
  package: 'SnakesAndLadders'
```

Now you can define the methods `tileNumber:` and `tileNumber`. This is not really nice because we should get a collection of tiles and now we put a number.

```
SLGame >> tileNumber: aNumber
  tiles := aNumber
```

```
SLGame >> tileNumber
  ^ tiles
```

These method definitions are enough to make our test pass. It means that our test was not really good because tiles should hold a collection containing the tiles and not just a number. We will address this point later.

18.6 A first real test

Since we would like to be able to check that our game is correct we can use its textual representation and test it as a way to check the game state. The following test should what we want.

```
SLGameTest >> testPrintingSimpleGame

  | game |
  game := SLGame new tileNumber: 12.
  self
    assert: game printString
    equals: '[1][2][3][4][5][6][7][8][9][10][11][12]'
```

What we would like is that the printing of the game asks the tiles to print themselves this way we will be able to take advantage that there will be different tiles in a modular way: i.e. we will not change the game to display the ladder and snake just have different tiles with different behavior.

The first step is then to define a class named `SLTile` as follows:

```
Object subclass: #SLTile
  instanceVariableNames: ''
  classVariableNames: ''
  package: 'SnakesAndLadders'
```

Now we would like to test the printing of a single tile. So let us define a test case named `SLTileTest`. This test case will test some basic behavior but it is nice to decompose our implementation process. We are trying to minimize the gap between one functionality and one test.

```
TestCase subclass: #SLTileTest
  instanceVariableNames: ''
  classVariableNames: ''
  package: 'SnakesAndLadders-Test'
```

Now we can write a simple test to make sure that we can print a tile.

```
SLTileTest >> testPrinting

  | tile |
  tile := SLTile new position: 6.
  self assert: tile printString equals: '[6]'
```

Tile position could have been managed by the game itself. But it means that we would have to ask the game for the position of a given tile and while it would work, it does not feel good. In Object-Oriented Design, we should distribute responsibilities to objects and their state is their first responsibility. Since the position is an attribute of a tile, better define it there.

This is where you see that the fact that the code is running is not a quality test for good Object-Oriented Design.

In particular it means that we should add an accessor to set the position and to add an instance variable position to the class SLile. Execute the test. You should get a debugger and use it to create a method position: as well as the instance variable.

Now we can define the printOn: method for tiles as follows. We add a [into the stream, then we asked the position to print itself in the stream by sending it the message printOn: and we add] in the stream. Since the position is a simple integer, the result of the position printOn: aStream expression is just to add a string representing the number in the stream.

```
SLTile >> printOn: aStream

  aStream << '['.
  position printOn: aStream.
  aStream << ']'
```

Your tile test should pass now. When we read the definition of the method printOn: above we see that it also sends the message printOn: here to the number used for the position. Indeed, we can send messages with the same name to different objects and each object may react differently to these messages. We can also send a message with the same name than the method to the receiver to perform a recursive call, but as with any recursive call we should have a non recursive branch.

We are ready to finish the printing of the game itself. Now we can define the method printOn: of the game to print all its tiles. Note that this will not work since so far we did not create tiles.

```
SLGame >> printOn: aStream

  tiles do: [ :aTile |
    aTile printOn: aStream ]
```

We modify the method `tileNumber:` to create an array of the given size and store it inside the `tiles` instance variable and to put a new tile for each position. Pay attention the tile should have the correct position.

```
SLGame >> tileNumber: aNumber
  ... Your code ...
```

Now your printing tests should be working both for the tile and the game. But wait if we run the test `testCheckingSimpleGame` it fails. Indeed we did not change the definition `tileNumber`. Do it and make sure that your tests all pass. And save your code.

18.7 Accessing one tile

Now we will need to be able to ask the game for a given tile, for example with the message `tileAt:`. Let us add a test for it.

```
SLGameTest >> testTileAt

  | game |
  game := SLGame new tileNumber: 12.
  self assert: (game tileAt: 6) printString equals: '[6]'
```

Define the method `tileAt:`.

```
SLGame >> tileAt: aNumber
  ... Your code ...
```

18.8 Adding players

Now we should add players. The first scenario to test is that when we add a player to game, it should be on the first tile.

Let us write a test: we create a game and a player. Then we add the player to the game and the player should be part of the players of the first tile.

```
SLGameTest >> testPlayerAtStart

  | game jill |
  game := SLGame new tileNumber: 12.
  jill := SLPlayer new name: 'Jill'.
  game addPlayer: jill.
  self assert: ((game tileAt: 1) players includes: jill).
```

```
Object subclass: #SLPlayer
  instanceVariableNames: 'name'
  classVariableNames: ''
  package: 'SnakesAndLadders'
```

Define the method name: in the class SLPlayer. Now we should think a bit how we should manage the players. We suspect that the game itself should get a list of players so that in the future it can ask each player to play its turn. Notice the previous sentence: we say each player to play and not the game to play the next turn - again this is Object-Oriented Design in action.

Now our test does not really cover the point that the game should keep track of the players so we will not do it. Similarly we may wonder if a player should know its position. At this point we do not know and we postpone this decision for another scenario.

```
SLGame >> addPlayer: aPlayer
  (tiles at: 1) addPlayer: aPlayer
```

Now what is clear is that a tile should keep a player list. Add an instance variable players to the SLTile class and initialize it to be an OrderedCollection.

```
SLTile >> initialize
  ... Your code ...
```

Then implement the method addPlayer:

```
SLTile >> addPlayer: aPlayer
  ... Your code ...
```

Now all your tests should pass.

Let us the opportunity to write better tests. We should check that we can add two players and that both are on the starting tile.

```
SLGameTest >> testSeveralPlayersAtStart

  | game jill jack |
  game := SLGame new tileNumber: 12.
  jill := SLPlayer new name: 'Jill'.
  jack := SLPlayer new name: 'Jack'.
  game addPlayer: jill.
  game addPlayer: jack.
  self assert: ((game tileAt: 1) players includes: jill).
  self assert: ((game tileAt: 1) players includes: jack).
```

All the tests should pass. This is the time to save and take a break.

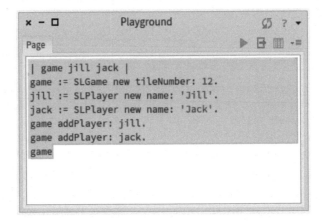

Figure 18-2 Playground in action. Use Do it and go - to get an embedded inspector.

18.9 Avoid leaking implementation information

We are not really happy with the previous tests for example testPlayerAt-Start.

```
SLGameTest >> testPlayerAtStart

    | game jill |
    game := SLGame new tileNumber: 12.
    jill := SLPlayer new name: 'Jill'.
    game addPlayer: jill.
    self assert: ((game tileAt: 1) players includes: jill).
```

Indeed a test is a first client of our code. Here we see in the expression play-ers includes: jill that we have to know that players are held in a collection and that this collection includes such a player.

It can be a real problem if later we decide to change how we manage players, since we will have to change all the places using the result of the players message.

Let us address this issue: define a method includesPlayer: that returns whether a tile has the given player.

```
SLTile >> includesPlayer: aPlayer
    ... Your code ...
```

Now we can rewrite the two tests testPlayerAtStart and testSever-alPlayersAtStart to use this new message.

```
SLGameTest >> testPlayerAtStart

    | game jill |
    game := SLGame new tileNumber: 12.
    jill := SLPlayer new name: 'Jill'.
    game addPlayer: jill.
    self assert: ((game tileAt: 1) includesPlayer: jill).
```

```
SLGameTest >> testSeveralPlayersAtStart

    | game jill jack |
    game := SLGame new tileNumber: 12.
    jill := SLPlayer new name: 'Jill'.
    jack := SLPlayer new name: 'Jack'.
    game addPlayer: jill.
    game addPlayer: jack.
    self assert: ((game tileAt: 1) includesPlayer: jill).
    self assert: ((game tileAt: 1) includesPlayer: jack).
```

18.10   About tools

Pharo is a living environment in which we can interact with the objects. Let us see a bit of that in action now.

Type the following game creation in a playground (as shown in Figure 18-2).

```
| game jill jack |
game := SLGame new tileNumber: 12.
jill := SLPlayer new name: 'Jill'.
jack := SLPlayer new name: 'Jack'.
game addPlayer: jill.
game addPlayer: jack.
game
```

Now you can inspect the game either using the inspect command-i or sending the message inspect to the game as in game inspect. You can also use the *do it and go* menu item of a playground window. You should get a picture similar to the one 18-3.

We see that the object is a SLGame instance and it has an instance variable named tiles. You can navigate on the instance variables as shown in Figure 18-4. Figure 18-5 shows that we can navigate the object structure: here we start from the game, go to the first tile and see the two players. At any moment you can interact with the selected object sending it messages.

18.11   Displaying players

Navigating the structure of the game is nice when we want to debug and interact with the game entities. Now we propose to display the player objects

Figure 18-3   Inspecting the game: a game instance and its instance variable `tiles`.

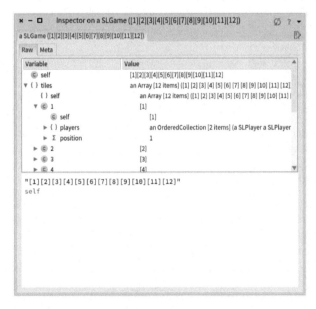

Figure 18-4   Navigating inside the game: getting inside the tiles and checking the players.

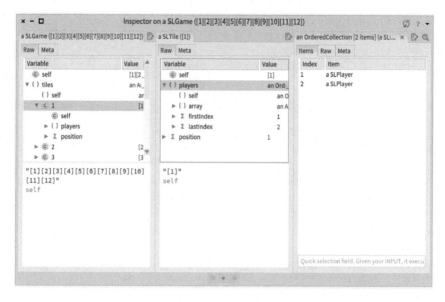

Figure 18-5 Navigating the objects using the navigation facilities of the inspector.

in a nicer way. We will reuse such behavior when printing the game to follow the movement of the player on the board.

Since we love testing, let us write a test describing what we expect when displaying a game.

```
SLGameTest >> testPrintingSimpleGameWithPlayers

    | game jill jack |
    game := SLGame new tileNumber: 12.
    jack := SLPlayer new name: 'Jack'.
    jill := SLPlayer new name: 'Jill'.
    game addPlayer: jill. "first player"
    game addPlayer: jack.
    self
        assert: game printString
        equals: '[1<Jill><Jack>][2][3][4][5][6][7][8][9][10][11][12]'
```

To make this test pass, you must define a printOn: on SLPlayer. Make sure that the printOn: of SLTile also invokes this new method.

```
SLPlayer >> printOn: aStream
    ... Your code ...
```

Here is a possible implementation for the tile logic.

```
SLTile >> printOn: aStream
  aStream << '['.
  position printOn: aStream.
  players do: [ :aPlayer | aPlayer printOn: aStream ].
  aStream << ']'
```

Run your tests, they should pass.

18.12   Preparing to move players

To move the player we need to know the tile on which it will arrive. We want
to ask the game: what is the target tile if this player (for example, jill) is moving a given distance. Let us write a test for the message tileFor: aPlayer
atDistance: aNumber.

```
SLGameTest >> testTileForAtDistance

  | jill game |
  game := SLGame new tileNumber: 12.
  jill := SLPlayer new name: 'Jill'.
  game addPlayer: jill.
  self assert: (game tileFor: jill atDistance: 4) position equals: 5.
```

What is implied is that a player should know its location or that the game
should start to look from the beginning to find what is the current position
of a player. The first option looks more reasonable in terms of efficiency and
this is the one we will implement.

Let us write a simpler test for the introduction of the position in a player.

```
SLGameTest >> testPlayerAtStartIsAtPosition1

  | game jill |
  game := SLGame new tileNumber: 12.
  jill := SLPlayer new name: 'Jill'.
  game addPlayer: jill.
  self assert: jill position equals: 1.
```

Define the methods position and position: in the class SLPlayer and add
an instance variable position to the class. If you run the test it should fail
saying that it got nil instead of one. This is normal because we never set the
position of a player. Modify the addPlayer: to handle this case.

```
SLGame >> addPlayer: aPlayer
  ... Your code ...
```

The test testPlayerAtStartIsAtPosition1 should now pass and we can
return to the testTileForAtDistance. Since we lost a bit track, the best
thing to do is to run our tests and check why they are failing. We get an error

saying that a game instance does not understand the message tileFor:at-Distance: this is normal since we never implemented it. For now we do not consider that a roll can bring the player further than the last tile.

Let us fix that now. Define the method tileFor:atDistance:

```
SLGame >> tileFor: aPlayer atDistance: aNumber
   ... Your code ...
```

Now all your test should pass and this is a good time to save your code.

18.13 Finding the tile of a player

We can start to move a player from a tile to another one. We should get the tile destination using the message tileFor:atDistance: and add the player there. Of course we should not forget that the tile where the player is currently positioned should be updated. So we need to know what is the tile of the player.

Now once a player has position it is then easy to find the tile on top of which it is. Let us write a test for it.

```
SLGameTest >> testTileOfPlayer

   | jill game |
   game := SLGame new tileNumber: 12.
   jill := SLPlayer new name: 'Jill'.
   game addPlayer: jill.
   self assert: (game tileOfPlayer: jill) position equals: 1.
```

Implement the method tileOfPlayer:.

```
SLGame >> tileOfPlayer: aSLPlayer
   ... Your code ...
```

18.14 Moving to another tile

Now we are ready to work on moving a player from one tile to the other. Let us express a test: we create only one player. We test that after the move, the new position is the one of the target tile, that the original tile does not have player and the target tile has effectively the player.

```
SLGameTest >> testMovePlayerADistance

   | jill game |
   game := SLGame new tileNumber: 12.
   jill := SLPlayer new name: 'Jill'.
   game addPlayer: jill.
   game movePlayer: jill distance: 4.
   self assert: jill position equals: 5.
```

```
self assert: (game tileAt: 1) players isEmpty.
self assert: ((game tileAt: 5) includesPlayer: jill).
```

What is hidden in this test is that we should be able to remove a player from a tile.

Since we should remove the player of a tile when it moves, implement the method

```
SLTile >> removePlayer: aPlayer
    ... Your code ...
```

Now propose an implementation of the method movePlayer: aPlayer distance: anInteger. You should get the destination tile for the player, remove the player from its current tile, add it to the destination tile and change the position of the player to reflect its new position.

```
SLGame >> movePlayer: aPlayer distance: anInteger
    ... Your code ...
```

We suspect that when we will introduce ladder and snake tiles, we will have to revisit this method because snakes and ladders do not store players just move them around.

About our implementation

The implementation that we propose below for the method movePlayer: aPlayer distance: anInteger is not as nice as we would like it to be. Why? Because it does not give a chance to the tiles to extend this behavior and our experience tells us that we will need it when we will introduce the snake and ladder. We will discuss that when we will arrive there.

```
SLGame >> movePlayer: aPlayer distance: anInteger
    | targetTile |
    targetTile := self tileFor: aPlayer atDistance: anInteger.
    (self tileOfPlayer: aPlayer) removePlayer: aPlayer.
    targetTile addPlayer: aPlayer.
    aPlayer position: targetTile position.
```

18.15 Snakes and ladders

Now we can introduce the two special tiles: the snakes and ladders. Let us analyse a bit their behavior: when a player lands on such a tile, it is automatically moved to another tile. As such, snake and ladder tiles do not need to keep references to players because players never stay on them.

Snakes is really similar to ladders: we could just have a special kind of tiles to manage them. Now we will define two separate classes so that we can add extra behavior. Remember creating a class is cheap. One behavior we will

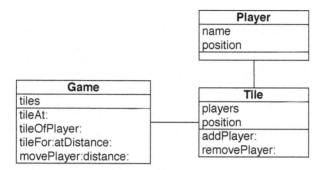

Figure 18-6   Current simple design: three classes with a player acting a simple object.

implement is a different printed version so that we can identify the kind of tile we have.

At the beginning of the chapter we used -> for ladders and <- for snakes.

```
[[1<Jill><Jack>][2->6][3][4][5][6][7->9][8][9][10][5<-11][12]
```

18.16   A hierarchy of tiles

We have now our default tile and two kinds of different *active* tiles. Now we will split our current tile class to be able to reuse a bit of its state and behavior with the new tiles. Our current tile class will then be one of the leaves of our hierarchy tree.

To factor the behavior of the active tiles, we will introduce a new class named ActiveTile. Once we will be done, we should have a hierarchy as the one presented in the Figure 18-7.

Let us start create the hierarchy.

Split Tile class in two

Let us do the following actions:

- Using the class refactoring "insert superclass" (click on the SLTile and check the class refactoring menu), introduce a new superclass to SLTile. Name it SLAbstractTile.

- Run the tests and they should pass.

- Using the class instance variable refactoring "pull up", push the position instance variable

- Run the tests and they should pass.

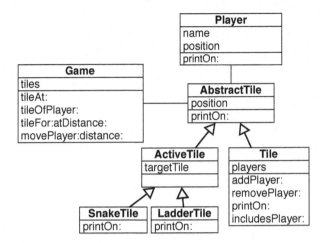

Figure 18-7 A hierarchy of tiles.

- Using the method refactoring "push up", push the methods `position` and `position:`.
- Run the tests and they should pass.

What you see is that we did not execute the actions randomly but we want to control that each step is under control using the tests.

Here are the classes and methods `printOn:`.

```
Object subclass: #SLAbstractTile
  instanceVariableNames: 'position'
  classVariableNames: ''
  package: 'SnakesAndLadders'
```

Define a `printOn:` method so that all the subclasses can be displayed in the board by their position.

```
SLAbstractTile >> printOn: aStream
  aStream << '['.
  position printOn: aStream.
  aStream << ']'
```

```
SLAbstractTile subclass: #SLTile
  instanceVariableNames: 'players'
  classVariableNames: ''
  package: 'SnakesAndLadders'
```

Adding snake and ladder tiles

Now we can add a new subclass to `SLAbstractTile`.

```
SLAbstractTile subclass: #SLActiveTile
  instanceVariableNames: 'targetTile'
  classVariableNames: ''
  package: 'SnakesAndLadders'
```

We add a method to: to set the destination tile.

```
SLActiveTile >> to: aTile
  targetTile := aTile
```

Then we add the two new subclasses of SLActiveTile

```
SLActiveTile subclass: #SLSnakeTile
  instanceVariableNames: ''
  classVariableNames: ''
  package: 'SnakesAndLadders'
```

```
SLSnakeTile >> printOn: aStream

  aStream << '['.
  targetTile position printOn: aStream.
  aStream << '<-'.
  position printOn: aStream.
  aStream << ']'
```

```
SLActiveTile subclass: #SLLadderTile
  instanceVariableNames: ''
  classVariableNames: ''
  package: 'SnakesAndLadders'
```

This is fun to see that the order when to print the position of the tile is different between the snakes and ladders.

```
SLLadderTile >> printOn: aStream

  aStream << '['.
  position printOn: aStream.
  aStream << '->'.
  targetTile position printOn: aStream.
  aStream << ']'
```

We did on purpose not to ask you to define tests to cover the changes. This exercise should show you how long sequence of programming without adding new tests expose us to potential bugs. They are often more stressful.

So let us add some tests to make sure that our code is correct.

```
SLTileTest >> testPrintingLadder

  | tile |
  tile := SLLadderTile new position: 2; to: (SLTile new position: 6).
  self assert: tile printString equals: '[2->6]'
```

```
SLTileTest >> testPrintingSnake

  | tile |
  tile := SLSnakeTile new position: 11; to: (SLTile new position: 5).
  self assert: tile printString equals: '[5<-11]'
```

Run the tests and they should pass. Save your code. Take a rest!

18.17 New printing hook

When we look at the printing situation we see code duplication logic. For example, we always see at least the repetition of the first and last expression.

```
SLTile >> printOn: aStream

  aStream << '['.
  position printOn: aStream.
  players do: [ :aPlayer | aPlayer printOn: aStream ].
  aStream << ']'
```

```
SLLadderTile >> printOn: aStream

  aStream << '['.
  position printOn: aStream.
  aStream << '->'.
  targetTile position printOn: aStream.
  aStream << ']'
```

Do you think that we can do better? What would be the solution?

In fact what we would like is to have a method that we can reuse and that handles the output of ' [ ] '. And in addition we would like to have another method for the contents between the parentheses and that we can specialize it. This way each class can define its own behavior for the inside part and reuse the parenthesis part.

This is what you will do now. Let us split the printOn: method of the class SLAbstractTile in two methods:

- a new method named printInsideOn: just printing the position, and

- the printOn: method using this new method.

```
SLAbstractTile >> printInsideOn: aStream

  position printOn: aStream
```

Now define the method printOn: to produce the same behavior as before but calling the message printInsideOn:.

```
SLAbstractTile >> printOn: aStream
  ... Your code ...
```

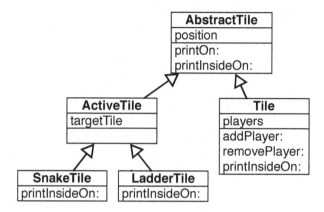

Figure 18-8 Introducing printInsideOn: as a new hook.

Run your tests and they should pass. You may have noticed that this is normal because none of them is covering the abstract tile. We should have been more picky on our tests.

What you should see is that we will have only one method defining the behavior of representing the surrounding of a tile and this is much better if one day we want to change it.

18.18 Using the new hook

Now you are ready to express the printing behavior of SLTile, SLSnake and SLLadder in a much more compact fashion. Do not forget to remove the printOn: methods in such classes, else they will hide the new behavior (If you do not get why you should read again the chapter on inheritance). You should get the situation depicted as in Figure 18-8.

Here is our definition for the printInsideOn: method of the class SLTile.

```
SLTile >> printInsideOn: aStream

  super printInsideOn: aStream.
  players do: [ :aPlayer | aPlayer printOn: aStream ].
```

What you should see is that we are invoking the default behavior (from the class SLAbstractTile) using the super pseudo-variable and we enrich it with the information of the players.

Define the one for the SLLadderTile class and the one for SLSnakeTile.

```
SLLadderTile >> printInsideOn: aStream
  ... Your code ...
```

```
SLSnakeTile >> printInsideOn: aStream
  ... Your code ...
```

super does not have to be the first expression

Now we show you our definition of `printInsideOn:` for the class `SLSnakeTile`. Why do we show it? Because it shows you that an expression invoking an overriden method can be placed anywhere. It does not have to be the first expression of a method. Here it is the last one.

```
SLSnakeTile >> printInsideOn: aStream

  targetTile position printOn: aStream.
  aStream << '<-'.
  super printInsideOn: aStream
```

Do not forget to run your tests. And they should all pass.

18.19 About hooks and templates

If we look at what we did. We created what is called a Hook/Template.

- The template method is the `printOn:` method. It defines a context of the execution of the hook methods.
- The `printInsideOn:` message is the hook that get specialized for each subclass. It happens in the context of a template method.

What you should see is that the `printOn:` message is also a hook of the `printString` message. There the `printString` method is creating a context and send the message `printOn:` which gets specialized.

The second point that we want to stress is that we turned expressions into a self-message. We transformed the expressions `position printOn: aStream` into `self printInsideOn: aStream` and such simple transformation created a point of variation extensible using inheritance. Note that the expression could have been a lot more complex.

Finally what is important to realize is that even `position printOn: aStream` creates a variation point. Imagine that we have multiple kind of positions, this expression will invoke the corresponding method on the object that is currently referred to by `position`. Such position objects could or not be organized in a hierarchy as soon as they offer a similar interface. So each message is in fact a variation point in a program.

18.20 Snake and ladder declaration

Now we should add to the game some messages to declare snake and ladder tiles. We propose to name the messages `setLadderFrom:to:` and `setSnake-`

From:to:. Now let us write a test and make sure that it fails before starting.

```
SLGameTest >> testFullGamePrintString

    | game |
    game := SLGame new tileNumber: 12.
    game
        setLadderFrom: 2 to: 6;
        setLadderFrom: 7 to: 9;
        setSnakeFrom: 11 to: 5.
    self
        assert: game printString
        equals: '[1][2->6][3][4][5][6][7->9][8][9][10][5<-11][12]'
```

Define the method setSnakerFrom:to: that takes two positions, the first one is the position of the tile and the second one is the position of the target. Pay attention that the message to: of the active tiles expects a tile and not a position.

```
SLGame >> setSnakeFrom: aSourcePosition to: aTargetPosition
    ... Your code ...
```

```
SLGame >> setLadderFrom: aSourcePosition to: aTargetPosition
    ... Your code ...
```

Run your tests! And save your code.

18.21 Better tile protocol

Now we should define what should happen when a player lands on an active tiles (snake or ladder). Indeed for the normal tiles, we implemented that the player change its position, then the origin tile loses the player and the receiving tile gains the player.

We implemented such behavior in the method movePlayer: aPlayer distance: anInteger shown below. We paid attention that a player cannot be in two places at the same time: we remove it from its tile, then move it to its destination.

```
SLGame >> movePlayer: aPlayer distance: anInteger
    | targetTile |
    targetTile := self tileFor: aPlayer atDistance: anInteger.
    (self tileOfPlayer: aPlayer) removePlayer: aPlayer.
    targetTile addPlayer: aPlayer.
    aPlayer position: targetTile position.
```

At that moment we said that we did not like too much this implementation. And now this is the time to understand why and do improve the situation.

First it would be good that the behavior to manage the entering and leaving of a tile would be closer to the objects performing it. We have two solutions:

we could move it to the tile or to the player class. Second we should take another factor into play: different tiles have different behavior; normal tiles manage players and active tiles are placing players on their target tile and they do not manage players. Therefore it is more interesting to define a variation point on the tile because we will be able to exploit it for normal and active tiles.

We propose to define two methods on the tile: one to accept a new player named acceptPlayer: and to release a player named releasePlayer:. Let us rewrite movePlayer: aPlayer distance: anInteger with such methods.

```
SLTile >> acceptPlayer: aPlayer
  self addPlayer: aPlayer.
  aPlayer position: position.
```

The use in this definition of self messages or direct instance variable access is an indication that definition belongs to this class. Now we define the method releasePlayer: as follows:

```
SLTile >> releasePlayer: aPlayer
  self removePlayer: aPlayer
```

Defining the method releasePlayer: was not necessary but we did it because it is more symmetrical.

Now we can redefine movePlayer: aPlayer distance: anInteger.

```
SLGame >> movePlayer: aPlayer distance: anInteger
  | targetTile |
  targetTile := self tileFor: aPlayer atDistance: anInteger.
  (self tileOfPlayer: aPlayer) releasePlayer: aPlayer.
  targetTile acceptPlayer: aPlayer.
```

All the tests should pass. And this is the power of test driven development, we change the implementation of our game and we can verify that we did not change its behavior.

Another little improvement

Now we can improve the definition of acceptPlayer:. We can implement its behavior partly on SLAbstractTile and partly on SLTile. This way the definition of the methods are closer to the definition of the instance variables and the state of the objects.

```
SLAbstractTile >> acceptPlayer: aPlayer
  aPlayer position: position
```

```
SLTile >> acceptPlayer: aPlayer
  super acceptPlayer: aPlayer.
  self addPlayer: aPlayer
```

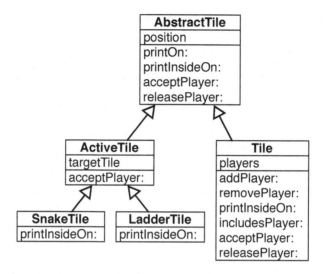

Figure 18-9   acceptPlayer: and releasePlayer: new message.

Note that we change the order of execution by invoking the superclass behavior first (using super acceptPlayer: aPlayer) because we prefer to invoke first the superclass method, because we prefer to think that a subclass is extending an existing behavior.

To be complete, we define that releasePlayer: does nothing on SLAbstractTile. We define it to document the two faces of the protocol. Figure 18-9 shows the situation.

```
SLAbstractTile >> releasePlayer: aPlayer
  "Do nothing by default, subclasses may modify this behavior."
```

18.22   Active tile actions

Now we are ready to implement the behavior of the active tiles. But.... yes we will write a test first. What we want to test is that when a player lands on a snake it falls back on the target and that the original tile does not have this player anymore. This is what this test expresses.

```
SLGameTest >> testPlayerStepOnASnake

  | jill game |
  game := SLGame new
      tileNumber: 12;
      setLadderFrom: 2 to: 6;
      setLadderFrom: 7 to: 9;
      setSnakeFrom: 11 to: 5.
```

```
jill := SLPlayer new name: 'Jill'.
game addPlayer: jill.
game movePlayer: jill distance: 10.
self assert: jill position equals: 5.
self assert: (game tileAt: 1) players isEmpty.
self assert: ((game tileAt: 5) includesPlayer: jill).
```

Now we just have to implement it!

```
SLActiveTile >> acceptPlayer: aPlayer
    ... Your code ...
```

There is nothing to do for the message releasePlayer:, because the player is never added to the active tile. Once you are done run the tests and save.

18.23 Alternating players

We are nearly finished with the game. First we should manage that each turn a different player is playing and that the game finishes when the current player lands on the final tile.

We would like to be able to:

- make the game play in automatic mode

- make the game one step at the time so that humans can play.

The logic for the automatic play can be expressed as follows:

```
play
   [ self isNotOver ] whileTrue: [
     self playPlayer: (self currentPlayer) roll: 6 atRandom ]
```

Until the game is finished, the game identifies the current player and plays this player for a given number given by a die of six faces. The expression 6 atRandom selects randomly a number between 1 and 6.

18.24 Player turns and current player

The game does not keep track of the players and their order. We will have to support it so that each player can play in alternance. It will also help us to compute the end of the game. Given a turn, we should identify the current player.

The following test verifies that we obtain the correct player for a given turn.

```
SLGameTest >> testCurrentPlayer

   | jack game jill |
   game := SLGame new tileNumber: 12.
   jack := SLPlayer new name: 'Jack'.
```

```
jill := SLPlayer new name: 'Jill'.
game addPlayer: jack; addPlayer: jill.
game turn: 1.
self assert: game currentPlayer equals: jack.
game turn: 2.
self assert: game currentPlayer equals: jill.
game turn: 3.
self assert: game currentPlayer equals: jack.
```

You should add two instance variables players and turn to the SLGame class.

Then you should initialize the two new instance variables adequately: the players instance variable to an OrderedCollection and the turn instance variable to zero.

```
SLGame >> initialize
  ... Your code ...
```

You should modify the method addPlayer: to add the player to the list of players as shown by the method below.

```
SLGame >> addPlayer: aPlayer
  aPlayer position: 1.
  players add: aPlayer.
  (tiles at: 1) addPlayer: aPlayer
```

We define also the setter method turn: to help us for the test. This is where you see that it would be good in Pharo to have the possibility to write tests inside the class and not to be forced to add a method definition just for a test but SUnit does not allow such behavior. One approach to resolve this, and ensuring only test code makes use of turn:, is to use class extensions. We make turn: belong to the *SnakesAndLadders-Test protocol. In this way if we only load the SnakesAndLadders package then it will not include any test specific methods.

```
SLGame >> turn: aNumber
  turn := aNumber
```

18.25 How to find the logic of currentPlayer?

Now we should define the method currentPlayer. We will try to show you how we brainstorm and experiment when we are looking for an algorithm or even the logic of a simple method.

Imagine a moment that we have two players Jack-Jill. The turns are the following ones: Jack 1, Jill 2, Jack 3, Jill 4, Jack 5.....

Now we know that we have two players. So using this information, at turn 5, the rest of the division of 5 by 2, gives us 1 so this is the turn of the first player. At turn 4, the rest of the division of 5 by 2 is zero so we take the latest player: Jill.

Here is an expression that shows the result when we have two players and we use the division.

```
(1 to: 10) collect: [ :each | each -> (each \\ 2) ]
> {1->1. 2->0. 3->1. 4->0. 5->1. 6->0. 7->1. 8->0. 9->1. 10->0}
```

Here is an expression that shows the result when we have three players and we use the division.

```
(1 to: 10) collect: [ :each | each -> (each \\ 3) ]
> {1->1. 2->2. 3->0. 4->1. 5->2. 6->0. 7->1. 8->2. 9->0. 10->1}
```

What you see is that each time we get 0, it means that this is the last player (second in the first case and third in the second).

This is what we do with the following method. We compute the rest of the division. We obtain a number between 0 and the player number minus one. This number indicates the index of the number in the players ordered collection. When it is zero it means that we should take the latest player.

```
SLGame >> currentPlayer

    | rest playerIndex |
    rest := (turn \\ players size).
    playerIndex := (rest isZero
            ifTrue: [ players size ]
            ifFalse: [ rest ]).
    ^ players at:   playerIndex
```

Run your tests and make sure that they all pass and save.

18.26 Game end

Checking for the end of the game can be implemented in at least two ways:

- the game can check if any of the player is on the last tile.
- or when a player lands on the last tile, its effect is to end the game.

We will implement the first solution but let us write a test first.

```
SLGameTest >> testIsOver

    | jack game |
    game := SLGame new tileNumber: 12.
    jack := SLPlayer new name: 'Jack'.
    game addPlayer: jack.
    self assert: jack position equals: 1.
    game movePlayer: jack distance: 11.
    self assert: jack position equals: 12.
```

```
  self assert: game isOver.
```

Now define the method isOver. You can use the anySatisfy: message which returns true if one of the elements of a collection (the receiver) satisfies a condition. The condition is that a player's position is the number of tiles (since the last tile position is equal to the number of tiles).

```
SLGame >> isOver
  ... Your code ...
```

Alternate solution

To implement the second version, we can introduce a new tile SLEndTile. Here is the list of what should be done:

- define a new class.

- redefine the acceptPlayer: to stop the game. Note that it means that the tile should have a reference to the game. This should be added to this special tile.

- initialize the last tile of the game to be an instance of such a class.

18.27   Playing one move

Before automating the play of the game we should make sure that a die roll will not bring our player outside the board.

Here is a simple test covering the situations.

```
SLGameTest >> testCanMoveToPosition

  | game |
  game := SLGame new tileNumber: 12.
  self assert: (game canMoveToPosition: 8).
  self assert: (game canMoveToPosition: 12).
  self deny: (game canMoveToPosition: 13).
```

Define the method canMoveToPosition:. It takes as input the position of the potential move.

```
SLGame >> canMoveToPosition: aNumber
  ... Your code ...
```

Playing one game step

Now we are finally ready to finish the implementation of the game. Here are two tests that check that the game can play a step correctly, i.e., picking the correct player and moving it in the correct place.

```
SLGameTest >> testPlayOneStep

  | jill jack game |
  game := SLGame new tileNumber: 12.
  jack := SLPlayer new name: 'Jack'.
  jill := SLPlayer new name: 'Jill'.
  game addPlayer: jill.
  game addPlayer: jack.
  self assert: jill position equals: 1.
  game playOneStepWithRoll: 3.
  self assert: jill position equals: 4.
  self assert: (game tileAt: 1) players size equals: 1.
  self assert: ((game tileAt: 4) includesPlayer: jill)
```

```
SLGameTest >> testPlayTwoSteps

  | jill jack game |
  game := SLGame new tileNumber: 12.
  jack := SLPlayer new name: 'Jack'.
  jill := SLPlayer new name: 'Jill'.
  game addPlayer: jill.
  game addPlayer: jack.
  game playOneStepWithRoll: 3.
  game playOneStepWithRoll: 2.
  "nothing changes for jill"
  self assert: jill position equals: 4.
  self assert: ((game tileAt: 4) includesPlayer: jill).
  "now let us verify that jack moved correctly to tile 3"
  self assert: (game tileAt: 1) players size equals: 0.
  self assert: jack position equals: 3.
  self assert: ((game tileAt: 3) includesPlayer: jack)
```

Here is a possible implementation of the method playOneStepWithRoll:.

```
SLGame >> playOneStepWithRoll: aNumber

  | currentPlayer |
  turn := turn + 1.
  currentPlayer := self currentPlayer.
  Transcript show: currentPlayer printString, 'drew ', aNumber
    printString, ': '.
  (self canMoveToPosition: currentPlayer position + aNumber)
    ifTrue: [ self movePlayer: currentPlayer distance: aNumber ].
  Transcript show: self; cr.
```

Now we can verify that when a player lands on a ladder it is getting up.

```
SLGameTest >> testPlayOneStepOnALadder

  | jill jack game |
  game := SLGame new
```

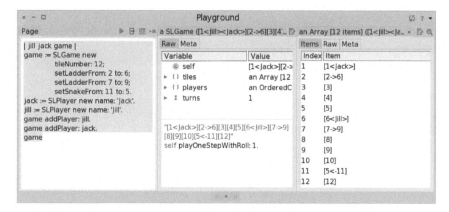

Figure 18-10 Playing step by step inside the inspector.

```
        tileNumber: 12;
        setLadderFrom: 2 to: 6;
        setLadderFrom: 7 to: 9;
        setSnakeFrom: 11 to: 5.
  jack := SLPlayer new name: 'Jack'.
  jill := SLPlayer new name: 'Jill'.
  game addPlayer: jill.
  game addPlayer: jack.
  game playOneStepWithRoll: 1.
  self assert: jill position equals: 6.
  self assert: (game tileAt: 1) players size equals: 1.
  self assert: ((game tileAt: 6) includesPlayer: jill).
```

You can try this method inside an inspector and see the result of the moves displayed in the transcript as shown in Figure 18-10.

```
| jill jack game |
game := SLGame new
      tileNumber: 12;
      setLadderFrom: 2 to: 6;
      setLadderFrom: 7 to: 9;
      setSnakeFrom: 11 to: 5.
jack := SLPlayer new name: 'Jack'.
jill := SLPlayer new name: 'Jill'.
game addPlayer: jill.
game addPlayer: jack.
game inspect
```

Figure 18-11 Automated play.

18.28 **Automated play**

Now we can can define the `play` method as follows and use it as shown in Figure 18-11.

```
SLGame >> play

  Transcript show: self; cr.
  [ self isOver not ] whileTrue: [
    self playOneStepWithRoll: 6 atRandom ]
```

Some final tests

We would like to make sure that the player is not moved when it does not land on the last tile or that the game is finished when one player lands on the last tile. Here are two tests covering such behavior.

```
SLGameTest >> testPlayOneStepOnExactFinish

  | jill jack game |
  game := SLGame new
      tileNumber: 12;
      setLadderFrom: 2 to: 6;
      setLadderFrom: 7 to: 9;
      setSnakeFrom: 11 to: 5.
  jack := SLPlayer new name: 'Jack'.
  jill := SLPlayer new name: 'Jill'.
  game addPlayer: jill.
  game addPlayer: jack.

  game playOneStepWithRoll: 11.
  "jill lands on the finish tile!"
  self assert: jill position equals: 12.
  self assert: (game tileAt: 1) players size equals: 1.
  self assert: ((game tileAt: 12) includesPlayer: jill).
```

```
  self assert: game isOver.

SLGameTest >> testPlayOneStepOnInexactFinish

  | jill jack game |
  game := SLGame new
      tileNumber: 12;
      setLadderFrom: 2 to: 6;
      setLadderFrom: 7 to: 9;
      setSnakeFrom: 11 to: 5.
  jack := SLPlayer new name: 'Jack'.
  jill := SLPlayer new name: 'Jill'.
  game addPlayer: jill.
  game addPlayer: jack.
    "jill moves"
  game playOneStepWithRoll: 9.
  self assert: jill position equals: 10.
  self assert: ((game tileAt: 10) includesPlayers: jill).
  "jack moves"
  game playOneStepWithRoll: 2.
  "jill tries to move but in fact stays at her place"
  game playOneStepWithRoll: 5.
  self assert: jill position equals: 10.
  self assert: ((game tileAt: 10) includesPlayer: jill).
  self deny: game isOver.
```

18.29 Variations

As you see this single game has multiple variations. Here are some of the ones you may want to implement:

- A player who lands on an occupied tile must go back to its originating tile.

- If you roll a number higher than the number of tiles needed to reach the last square, you must continue moving backwards from the end.

You will see that such extensions can be implemented in different manner. We suggest to avoid conditions but define objects responsible for this behavior and its variations.

18.30 Conclusion

This chapter went step by step to the process of getting from requirements to an actual implementation covered by tests.

This chapter shows that design is an iterative process. What is also important is that without tests we would be a lot more worried about breaking something without be warned immediately. With tests we were able to change some parts of the design and rapidly make sure that the previous specification still hold.

This chapter shows that identifying objects and their interactions is not always straightforward and multiple designs are often valid.

CHAPTER **19**

TinyChat: a fun and small chat client/server

Pharo allows the definition of a REST server in a couple of lines of code thanks to the Teapot package by zeroflag, which extends the superb HTTP client/server Zinc developed by BetaNine and was given to the community. The goal of this chapter is to make you develop, in five small classes, a client/server chat application with a graphical client. This little adventure will familiarize you with Pharo and show the ease with which Pharo lets you define a REST server. Developed in a couple of hours, TinyChat has been designed as a pedagogical application. At the end of the chapter, we propose a list of possible improvements.

TinyChat has been developed by O. Auverlot and S. Ducasse with a lot of fun.

19.1 Objectives and architecture

We are going to build a chat server and one graphical client as shown in Figure 19-1.

The communication between the client and the server will be based on HTTP and REST. In addition to the classes TCServer and TinyChat (the client), we will define three other classes: TCMessage which represents exchanged messages (as a future exercise you could extend TinyChat to use more structured elements such as JSON or STON (the Pharo object format), TCMessageQueue which stores messages, and TCConsole the graphical interface.

Figure 19-1 Chatting with TinyChat.

19.2 Loading Teapot

We can load Teapot using the Configuration Browser, which you can find in the Tools menu item of the main menu. Select Teapot and click "Install Stable". Another solution is to use the following script:

```
Gofer it
    smalltalkhubUser: 'zeroflag' project: 'Teapot';
    configuration;
    loadStable.
```

Now we are ready to start.

19.3 Message representation

A message is a really simple object with a text and sender identifier.

Class TCMessage

We define the class TCMessage in the package TinyChat.

```
Object subclass: #TCMessage
  instanceVariableNames: 'sender text separator'
  classVariableNames: ''
  category: 'TinyChat'
```

The instance variables are as follows:

- sender: the identifier of the sender,

- text: the message text, and

- separator: a character to separate the sender and the text.

Accessor creation

We create the following accessors:

```
TCMessage >> sender
  ^ sender

TCMessage >> sender: anObject
  sender := anObject

TCMessage >> text
  ^ text

TCMessage >> text: anObject
  text := anObject
```

19.4   Instance initialisation

Each time an instance is created, its initialize method is invoked. We re-define this method to set the separator value to the string >.

```
TCMessage >> initialize
  super initialize.
  separator := '>'.
```

Now we create a class method named from:text: to instantiate a message (a class method is a method that will be executed on a class and not on an instance of this class):

```
TCMessage class >> from: aSender text: aText
  ^ self new sender: aSender; text: aText; yourself
```

The message yourself returns the message receiver: this way we ensure that the returned object is the new instance and not the value returned by the text: message. This definition is equivalent to the following:

```
TCMessage class >> from: aSender text: aText
  | instance |
  instance := self new.
  instance sender: aSender; text: aText.
  ^ instance
```

19.5   Converting a message object into a string

We add the method printOn: to transform a message object into a character string. The model we use is sender-separator-text-crlf. Example: 'john>hello !!!'. The method printOn: is automatically invoked by the method printString. This method is invoked by tools such as the debugger or object inspector.

```
TCMessage >> printOn: aStream

  aStream
    << self sender; << separator;
    << self text; << String crlf
```

19.6 Building a message from a string

We also define two methods to create a message object from a plain string of the form: `'olivier>tinychat is cool'`.

First we create the method `fromString:` filling up the instance variables of an instance. It will be invoked like this: `TCMessage new fromString: 'olivier>tinychat is cool'`, then the class method `fromString:` which will first create the instance.

```
TCMessage >> fromString: aString
  "Compose a message from a string of this form 'sender>message'."
  | items |
  items := aString subStrings: separator.
  self sender: items first.
  self text: items second.
```

You can test the instance method with the following expression `TCMessage new fromString: 'olivier>tinychat is cool'`.

```
TCMessage class >> fromString: aString
  ^ self new
    fromString: aString;
    yourself
```

When you execute the following expression `TCMessage fromString: 'olivier>tiny chat is cool'` you should get a message. We are now ready to work on the server.

19.7 Starting with the server

For the server, we are going to define a class to manage a message queue. This is not really mandatory but it allows us to separate responsibilities.

Storing messages

Create the class `TCMessageQueue` in the package *TinyChat-Server*.

```
Object subclass: #TCMessageQueue
  instanceVariableNames: 'messages'
  classVariableNames: ''
  category: 'TinyChat-server'
```

The messages instance variable is an ordered collection whose elements are instances TCMessage. An OrderedCollection is a collection which dynamically grows when elements are added to it. We add an instance initialize method so that each new instance gets a proper messages collection.

```
TCMessageQueue >> initialize
  super initialize.
  messages := OrderedCollection new.
```

Basic operations on message list

We should be able to add, clear the list, and count the number of messages, so we define three methods: add:, reset, and size.

```
TCMessageQueue >> add: aMessage
  messages add: aMessage

TCMessageQueue >> reset
  messages removeAll

TCMessageQueue >> size
  ^ messages size
```

List of messages from a position

When a client asks the server about the list of the last exchanged messages, it mentions the index of the last message it knows. The server then answers the list of messages received since this index.

```
TCMessageQueue >> listFrom: aIndex
  ^ (aIndex > 0 and: [ aIndex <= messages size])
    ifTrue: [ messages copyFrom: aIndex to: messages size ]
    ifFalse: [ #() ]
```

Message formatting

The server should be able to transfer a list of messages to its client given an index. We add the possibility to format a list of messages (given an index). We define the method formattedMessagesFrom: using the formatting of a single message as follows:

```
TCMessageQueue >> formattedMessagesFrom: aMessageNumber

  ^ String streamContents: [ :formattedMessagesStream |
    (self listFrom: aMessageNumber)
      do: [ :m | formattedMessagesStream << m printString ]
    ]
```

Note how the streamContents: lets us manipulate a stream of characters.

19.8 The Chat server

The core of the server is based on the Teapot REST framework. It supports the sending and receiving of messages. In addition this server keeps a list of messages that it communicates to clients.

TCServer class creation

We create the class TCServer in the *TinyChat-Server* package.

```
Object subclass: #TCServer
  instanceVariableNames: 'teapotServer messagesQueue'
  classVariableNames: ''
  category: 'TinyChat-Server'
```

The instance variable messagesQueue represents the list of received and sent messages. We initialize it like this:

```
TCServer >> initialize
  super initialize.
  messagesQueue := TCMessageQueue new.
```

The instance variable teapotServer refers to an instance of the Teapot server that we will create using the method initializePort:

```
TCServer >> initializePort: anInteger
  teapotServer := Teapot configure: {
    #defaultOutput -> #text.
    #port -> anInteger.
    #debugMode -> true
  }.
  teapotServer start.
```

The HTTP routes are defined in the method registerRoutes. Three operations are defined:

- GET messages/count: returns to the client the number of messages received by the server,

- GET messages/<id:IsInteger>: the server returns messages from an index, and

- POST /message/add: the client sends a new message to the server.

```
TCServer >> registerRoutes
  teapotServer
    GET: '/messages/count' -> (Send message: #messageCount to: self);
    GET: '/messages/<id:IsInteger>' -> (Send message: #messagesFrom:
    to: self);
    POST: '/messages/add' -> (Send message: #addMessage: to: self)
```

Here we express that the path `message/count` will execute the message messageCount on the server itself. The pattern `<id:IsInteger>` indicates that the argument should be expressed as number and that it will be converted into an integer.

Error handling is managed in the method `registerErrorHandlers`. Here we see how we can get an instance of the class `TeaResponse`.

```
TCServer >> registerErrorHandlers
  teapotServer
    exception: KeyNotFound -> (TeaResponse notFound body: 'No such
    message')
```

Starting the server is done in the class method `TCServer class>>startOn:` that gets the TCP port as argument.

```
TCServer class >> startOn: aPortNumber
  ^self new
    initializePort: aPortNumber;
    registerRoutes;
    registerErrorHandlers;
    yourself
```

We should also offer the possibility to stop the server. The method `stop` stops the teapot server and empties the message list.

```
TCServer >> stop
  teapotServer stop.
  messagesQueue reset.
```

Since there is a chance that you may execute the expression `TCServer startOn:` multiple times, we define the class method `stopAll` which stops all the servers by iterating over all the instances of the class `TCServer`. The method `TCServer class>>stopAll` stops each server.

```
TCServer class >> stopAll
  self allInstancesDo: #stop
```

19.9 Server logic

Now we should define the logic of the server. We define a method `addMessage` that extracts the message from the request. It adds a newly created message (instance of class `TCMessage`) to the list of messages.

```
TCServer >> addMessage: aRequest
  messagesQueue add: (TCMessage from: (aRequest at: #sender) text:
    (aRequest at: #text)).
```

The method `messageCount` gives the number of received messages.

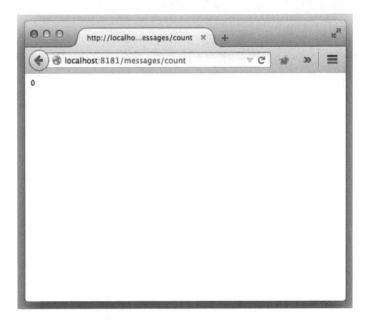

Figure 19-2 Testing the server.

```
TCServer >> messageCount
    ^ messagesQueue size
```

The method messageFrom: gives the list of messages received by the server since a given index (specified by the client). The messages returned to the client are a string of characters. This is definitively a point to improve - using string is a poor choice here.

```
TCServer >> messagesFrom: request
    ^ messagesQueue formattedMessagesFrom: (request at: #id)
```

Now the server is finished and we can test it. First let us begin by starting it:

```
    TCServer startOn: 8181
```

Now we can verify that it is running either with a web browser (Figure 19-2), or with a Zinc expression as follows:

```
ZnClient new url: 'http://localhost:8181/messages/count' ; get
```

Shell lovers can also use the curl command:

```
    curl http://localhost:8181/messages/count
```

We can also add a message the following way:

```
ZnClient new
  url: 'http://localhost:8181/messages/add';
  formAt: 'sender' put: 'olivier';
  formAt: 'text' put: 'Super cool ce tinychat' ; post
```

19.10   The client

Now we can concentrate on the client part of TinyChat. We decomposed the client into two classes:

- TinyChat is the class that defines the connection logic (connection, send, and message reception),
- TCConsole is a class defining the user interface.

The logic of the client is:

- During client startup, it asks the server the index of the last received message,
- Every two seconds, it requests from the server the messages exchanged since its last connection. To do so, it passes to the server the index of the last message it got.

TinyChat class

We now define the class TinyChat in the package TinyChat-client.

```
Object subclass: #TinyChat
  instanceVariableNames: 'url login exit messages console
    lastMessageIndex'
  classVariableNames: ''
  category: 'TinyChat-client'
```

This class defines the following instance variables:

- url that contains the server url,
- login a string identifying the client,
- messages is an ordered collection containing the messages read by the client,
- lastMessageIndex is the index of the last message read by the client,
- exit controls the connection. While exit is false, the client regularly connects to the server to get the unread messages
- console refers to the graphical console that allows the user to enter and read messages.

We initialize these variables in the following instance initialize method.

```
TinyChat >> initialize
  super initialize.
  exit := false.
  lastMessageIndex := 0.
  messages := OrderedCollection new.
```

HTTP commands

Now, we define methods to communicate with the server. They are based on the HTTP protocol. Two methods will format the request. One, which does not take an argument, builds the requests /messages/add and /messages/count. The other has an argument used to get the message given a position.

```
TinyChat >> command: aPath
  ^'{1}{2}' format: { url . aPath }

TinyChat >> command: aPath argument: anArgument
  ^'{1}{2}/{3}' format: { url . aPath . anArgument asString }
```

Now that we have these low-level operations we can define the three HTTP commands of the client as follows:

```
TinyChat >> cmdLastMessageID
  ^ self command: '/messages/count'

TinyChat >> cmdNewMessage
  ^self command: '/messages/add'

TinyChat >> cmdMessagesFromLastIndexToEnd
  "Returns the server messages from my current last index to the
    last one on the server."
  ^ self command: '/messages' argument: lastMessageIndex
```

Now we can create commands but we need to emit them. This is what we look at now.

19.11 Client operations

We need to send the commands to the server and to get back information from the server. We define two methods. The method readLastMessageID returns the index of the last message received from the server.

```
TinyChat >> readLastMessageID
  | id |
  id := (ZnClient new url: self cmdLastMessageID; get) asInteger.
  id = 0 ifTrue: [ id := 1 ].
  ^ id
```

The method `readMissingMessages` adds the last messages received from the server to the list of messages known by the client. This method returns the number of received messages.

```
TinyChat >> readMissingMessages
  "Gets the new messages that have been posted since the last
    request."
  | response receivedMessages |
  response := (ZnClient new url: self cmdMessagesFromLastIndexToEnd;
    get).
  ^ response
    ifNil: [ 0 ]
    ifNotNil: [
      receivedMessages := response subStrings: (String crlf).
      receivedMessages do: [ :msg | messages add: (TCMessage
    fromString: msg) ].
      receivedMessages size.
    ].
```

We are now ready to define the refresh behavior of the client via the method `refreshMessages`. It uses a light process to read the messages received from the server at a regular interval. The delay is set to 2 seconds. (The message `fork` sent to a block (a lexical closure in Pharo) executes this block in a light process). The logic of this method is to loop as long as the client does not specify to stop via the state of the `exit` variable.

The expression `(Delay forSeconds: 2) wait` suspends the execution of the process in which it is executed for a given number of seconds.

```
TinyChat >> refreshMessages
  [
    [ exit ] whileFalse: [
      (Delay forSeconds: 2) wait.
      lastMessageIndex := lastMessageIndex + (self
    readMissingMessages).
      console print: messages.
    ]
  ] fork
```

The method `sendNewMessage:` posts the message written by the client to the server.

```
TinyChat >> sendNewMessage: aMessage
  ^ ZnClient new
    url: self cmdNewMessage;
    formAt: 'sender' put: (aMessage sender);
    formAt: 'text' put: (aMessage text);
    post
```

This method is used by the method `send:` that gets the text written by the user. The string is converted into an instance of `TCMessage`. The message is sent and the client updates the index of the last message it knows, then it prints the message in the graphical interface.

```
TinyChat >> send: aString
  "When we send a message, we push it to the server and in addition
    we update the local list of posted messages."

  | msg |
  msg := TCMessage from: login text: aString.
  self sendNewMessage: msg.
  lastMessageIndex := lastMessageIndex + (self readMissingMessages).
  console print: messages.
```

We should also handle the server disconnection. We define the method dis-connect that sends a message to the client indicating that it is disconnecting and also stops the connecting loop of the server by putting exit to true.

```
TinyChat >> disconnect
  self sendNewMessage: (TCMessage from: login text: 'I exited from
    the chat room.').
  exit := true
```

19.12 Client connection parameters

Since the client should contact the server on specific ports, we define a method to initialize the connection parameters. We define the class method Tiny-Chat class>>connect:port:login: so that we can connect the following way to the server: TinyChat connect: 'localhost' port: 8080 login: 'username'

```
TinyChat class >> connect: aHost port: aPort login: aLogin

  ^ self new
    host: aHost port: aPort login: aLogin;
    start
```

TinyChat class>>connect:port:login: uses the method host:port:lo-gin:. This method just updates the url instance variable and sets the login as specified.

```
TinyChat >> host: aHost port: aPort login: aLogin
  url := 'http://' , aHost , ':' , aPort asString.
  login := aLogin
```

Finally we define a method start: which creates a graphical console (that we will define later), tells the server that there is a new client, and gets the last message received by the server. Note that a good evolution would be to decouple the model from its user interface by using notifications.

```
TinyChat >> start
  console := TCConsole attach: self.
  self sendNewMessage: (TCMessage from: login text: 'I joined the
    chat room').
  lastMessageIndex := self readLastMessageID.
  self refreshMessages.
```

19.13 User interface

The user interface is composed of a window with a list and an input field as shown in Figure 19-1.

```
ComposableModel subclass: #TCConsole
  instanceVariableNames: 'chat list input'
  classVariableNames: ''
  category: 'TinyChat-client'
```

Note that the class TCConsole inherits from ComposableModel. This class is the root of the user interface logic classes. TCConsole defines the logic of the client interface (i.e. what happens when we enter text in the input field...). Based on the information given in this class, the Spec user interface builder automatically builds the visual representation. The chat instance variable is a reference to an instance of the client model TinyChat and requires a setter method (chat:). The list and input instance variables both require an accessor. This is required by the User Interface builder.

```
TCConsole >> input
  ^ input

TCConsole >> list
  ^ list

TCConsole >> chat: anObject
  chat := anObject
```

We set the title of the window by defining the method title.

```
TCConsole >> title
  ^ 'TinyChat'
```

Now we should specify the layout of the graphical elements that compose the client. To do so we define the class method TCConsole class>>default-Spec. Here we need a column with a list and an input field placed right below.

```
TCConsole class >> defaultSpec
  <spec: #default>

  ^ SpecLayout composed
    newColumn: [ :c |
```

```
    c add: #list; add: #input height: 30 ]; yourself
```

We should now initialize the widgets that we will use. The method initial-izeWidgets specifies the nature and behavior of the graphical components. The message acceptBlock: defines the action to be executed then the text is entered in the input field. Here we send it to the chat model and empty it.

```
TCConsole >> initializeWidgets

  list := ListModel new.
  input := TextInputFieldModel new
    ghostText: 'Type your message here...';
    enabled: true;
    acceptBlock: [ :string |
      chat send: string.
      input text: '' ].
  self focusOrder add: input.
```

The method print displays the messages received by the client and assigns them to the list contents.

```
TCConsole >> print: aCollectionOfMessages
  list items: (aCollectionOfMessages collect: [ :m | m printString
    ])
```

Note that this method is invoked by the method refreshMessages and that changing all the list elements when we add just one element is rather ugly but ok for now.

Finally we need to define the class method TCConsole class>>attach: that gets the client model as argument. This method opens the graphical elements and puts in place a mechanism that will close the connection as soon as the client closes the window.

```
TCConsole class >> attach: aTinyChat
  | window |
  window := self new chat: aTinyChat.
  window openWithSpec whenClosedDo: [ aTinyChat disconnect ].
  ^ window
```

19.14 Now chatting

Now you can chat with your server. The example resets the server and opens two clients.

```
| tco tcs |
TCServer stopAll.
TCServer startOn: 8080.
tco := TinyChat connect: 'localhost' port: 8080 login: 'olivier'.
tco send: 'hello'.
tcs := TinyChat connect: 'localhost' port: 8080 login: 'Stef'.
```

Figure 19-3   Server access.

```
tcs send: 'salut olivier'
```

19.15   Conclusion and ideas for future extensions

We show that creating a REST server is really simple with Teapot. TinyChat provides a fun context to explore programming in Pharo and we hope that you like it. We designed TinyChat so that it favors extensions and exploration. Here is a list of possible extensions.

- Using JSON or STON to exchange information and not plain strings.
- Making sure that the clients can handle a failure of the server.
- Adding only the necessary messages to the list in the graphical client.
- Managing concurrent access in the server message collection (if the server should handle concurrent requests the current implementation is not correct).
- Managing connection errors.
- Getting the list of connected users.
- Editing the delay to check for new messages.

There are probably more extensions and we hope that you will have fun exploring some. The code of the project is available at http://www.smalltalkhub.com/#!/~olivierauverlot/TinyChat.